W9-AAT-703

Queen Isabella
and the
Unification
of Spain

Queen Isabella and the Unification of Spain

Nancy Whitelaw

MORGAN
REYNOLDS
Publishing, Inc.

620 South Elm Street, Suite 223
Greensboro, North Carolina 27406
http://www.morganreynolds.com

European Queens

Queen Isabella
Catherine de' Medici
Catherine the Great
Marie Antoinette
Queen Victoria

QUEEN ISABELLA AND THE UNIFICATION OF SPAIN

Library of Congress Cataloging-in-Publication Data

Whitelaw, Nancy.
Queen Isabella and the unification of Spain / Nancy Whitelaw.— 1st ed.
p. cm. — (European queens)
Includes bibliographical references and index.
ISBN 1-931798-25-7 (library binding)
1. Isabella I, Queen of Spain, 1451-1504—Juvenile literature. 2.
Spain—History—Ferdinand and Isabella, 1479-1516—Juvenile literature. 3.
Queens—Spain—Biography—Juvenile literature. I. Title. II. Series.
DP163.W45 2004
946'.03'092—dc22

2004014715

Printed in the United States of America
First Edition

Contents

1

A Weak King

King Enrique IV, ruler of Castile and León, certainly looked like a strong king. Tall and blond, with piercing blue eyes, he was a strikingly handsome man. Unfortunately, looks are often deceiving. King Enrique was actually a weak, lazy monarch who preferred hunting and gambling to the hard work of politics and diplomacy. He lived in fear of the powerful nobility that posed a constant threat to his throne and his life. He tried to buy their support with gifts of land and money that drained the treasury and forced him to raise taxes. Although from 1454-1474 Enrique ruled over the largest and most powerful kingdom on the Iberian Peninsula, he spent most of his time hosting parties and roaming the heavily wooded forests of his lands. He was seldom in the capital city of Segovia. He married twice, but

Opposite: Queen Isabella of Castile. *(Courtesy of Art Resource.)*

Enrique IV, Isabella's half-brother.

showed little interest in his wives or any other women. When his second wife finally produced a daughter, most of the kingdom called the girl Juana la Beltraneja because they believed that Don Beltran de la Cueva, a powerful noble, was her real father.

Enrique had a younger half-sister, the beautiful blue-eyed Princess Isabella, and a younger half-brother, Prince Alfonso. Isabella and Alfonso lived with Enrique because their insane mother was confined to a castle far away. When their father died, Enrique had promised to care for them and he had kept his word. But he suspected that a rebellion was in the offing and began to worry he would be replaced by the young prince Alfonso. Enrique planned to pass his kingdom to his daughter, but he heard the whispers that La Beltraneja did not have a legal claim to the throne because she was not his legitimate child.

Enrique had good reason to fear a plot against him. The people of his kingdom were unhappy. Groups of rebellious citizens gathered in the streets and in public buildings to criticize Enrique for poor financial management, favoritism toward the wealthy, high taxes, widespread hunger, and the corrupt

Princess Isabella of Castile.

justice system. Enrique escaped the crowds, and his responsibilities, by going into the woods to hunt as often as possible.

The calls for a new ruler grew louder. Enrique decided to try to get his half-sister Isabella out of the country, away from any conspirators who might try to put her on his throne. He proposed that the thirteen-year-old princess marry thirty-two-year-old King Afonso V of Portugal, a rich widower. This marriage, like other royal marriages, would be arranged to serve political goals. It would remove Isabella from Castile, and it would unite the kingdoms of Portugal and Castile, which would provide Enrique more money and power.

Enrique considered his marriageable half-sister to be a valuable bargaining tool. He probably never considered the possibility that Isabella would refuse to be his pawn. It was the fate of every woman of royal birth to have a political marriage planned for her. But young Isabella was not like most princesses. She declared that she would not marry King Afonso and reminded Enrique that her father's will stated she could not be married off without the consent of the nobles of the realm. Because many of those nobles were not friendly toward Enrique, Isabella knew they would take her side in order to prevent Enrique from gaining more power.

Enrique had to admit that Isabella was right. He did not want to give his enemies any reason to take away his throne. He called off the marriage and sent Isabella away to Segovia, where he kept her under heavy guard. He made a half-hearted attempt to appease the rebels in his kingdoms by promising free elections, the abolition of taxation without representation, restraints on the power of judges, and more authority for the clergy. He even kept his promises for almost two weeks.

By 1465, rebels had resumed their demonstrations against Enrique, roaming from village to village destroying crops and cattle. Each side worked to win the support of individual towns and powerful nobles. Isabella's friend and protector, Archbishop Alfonso Carrillo de Acuña, led a coalition of rebels that dethroned a mannequin of Enrique in a mock ceremony that raised Prince Alfonso, Isabella's brother, to the throne in his place. Across the country, people swore their allegiance to the eleven-year-old king. Enrique's situation was growing more desperate.

Enrique's supporters feared the country would soon buckle under the strain of this simmering civil war. They urged him to confront the rebellion head-on, but he refused to take decisive action. Alfonso's faction grew stronger as more and more people pinned their hopes for a better life on the beautiful little boy. In the fifteenth

Prince Alfonso, Isabella's younger brother.

century, most people believed in supernatural powers and that miracles were possible. Young Prince Alfonso seemed to offer the possibility of a better world.

In April 1466, Enrique accepted another marriage proposal for Isabella. This one came from forty-three-year-old Pedro Giron, master of a military brotherhood in Castile. Giron promised Enrique he could persuade the rebels to stop fighting. All he wanted in return was Princess Isabella's hand in marriage.

Isabella had heard rumors that Giron was foul-mouthed, vain, and had a reputation for infidelity. A devout Catholic, she shuddered at the prospect of marrying such a man. This time she knew the nobles would not intervene on her behalf—they too wanted to avoid all-out civil war and believed her marriage to Giron would decrease the tension. Isabella could only hope that God would somehow intervene. She cloistered herself in her room and began to pray.

Just a few days before the betrothal ceremony was scheduled, the news arrived that Giron had died while on his way to his young bride. Some suspected poison, others believed it was divine intervention. Isabella said nothing publicly. She only continued to pray. She spent another year locked away in Segovia, unable to see her brother or her mother, wondering only what would happen next. Outside the gates, the rebels continued their fight. She heard news of pitched battles between loyalists and rebels that resulted in many deaths and injuries but no clear winner.

In the fall of 1467, some of Enrique's most trusted aides betrayed him. They opened the gates of Segovia to the rebels, and Isabella was free at last. She went immediately to her mother, where her brother soon joined them. Isabella supported Alfonso over Enrique, but she had not yet publicly declared her allegiance. She thought it would be wiser not to let her feelings become known. If she remained neutral she might avoid being seized by Enrique's supporters. Isabella asked the king, her half-brother, for a guarantee

A view of the alcazar of Segovia where Isabella was held.

of safety. He granted it, calling her his "dear and much loved sister."

Though Isabella doubted his sincerity, she hoped his words would make her safe from attack by his supporters. She took refuge in a convent while Alfonso toured neighboring regions hoping to energize his supporters.

Although Isabella quietly supported Alfonso's claim to the throne, she disapproved of his attempts to seize power. She accepted that Enrique, their father's eldest son, was the rightful heir to the throne. Alfonso should not try to break the line of royal succession. He should take the throne only when Enrique could no longer rule. She prayed long and often, frequently calling on God to restore the throne of all Castile to Enrique. Let Alfonso take his turn, she prayed, when his time came.

In early July 1468, messengers pounded on the door of the convent. They brought news that Isabella could hardly believe. Alfonso had been found in a deep coma. A few days later, he died.

No one knows what killed Alfonso. The dreaded Black Death was sweeping across the Iberian Peninsula, but Isabella learned that her brother had not exhibited any of the plague's telltale pus-filled sores. Her advisors feared that Alfonso had been poisoned. They would not allow her to attend his funeral out of fear that she would be taken into custody by King Enrique. She stayed in the convent, grieving alone. Isabella wondered if perhaps Alfonso's death was a message from God that he was not the rightful heir; if his death was his punishment for challenging the throne.

Soon after Alfonso's death, one of Isabella's advisors, Archbishop Carrillo, came to see her. Politeness forbade her to refuse him. He spent little time on condolences; he had an important message. He and other supporters of the late Alfonso wanted her to take the throne of Castile.

Isabella might have been tempted to accept the offer. But her temptation was overridden by her sense of what was right. She could not become queen while Enrique, the rightful heir, was alive. Behind this lofty sentiment was a more practical realization: there was little political support for her own coronation. Although three women had ruled Castile before, they had all been widows of kings who were

Isabella's advisor, the Archbishop Carrillo.

firmly ensconced in power. She told Carrillo she could not accept his offer.

Without a candidate to champion, the rebels sent out the message that they would stop fighting if Enrique would promise to recognize Isabella as his heir after he died. Enrique met with Isabella and Archbishop Carrillo in August of 1468 to discuss the succession. He and Isabella embraced warmly and both expressed their desire for peace. Isabella promised to respect Enrique as her king. Enrique promised that Isabella, not La Beltraneja, would be his heir to the throne. He awarded her seven small towns in Castile as a token of his sincerity. She would receive Madrid, a large city in the central plateau, in a year if all went well. The gifting of cities and towns was one way the royal family earned money— rule of a town gave access to its tax revenue.

Enrique also promised not to force Isabella to marry against her will, and Isabella promised not to marry without

Enrique's approval. The agreement, later called the Toros de Guisandro, seemed like a perfect solution to both their personal and political conflicts.

The public signing of the treaty was a grand affair. Hundreds of witnesses gathered to hear the document read aloud. Clergy, nobility, and commoners kissed the princess's hand as a sign of loyalty and an apostolic blessing was given. As trumpets blared, the people cheered. The civil war was over. The future for Isabella as queen of Castile was assured by God and man.

Isabella was somewhat renewed in spirit after the ceremony. Although still in mourning for Alfonso, she had a new challenge to focus her attention. She would continue to study history and government, and to meditate and pray. When her time to rule came she planned to be a worthy queen.

A year later, King Juan II of Aragón proposed that Isabella marry his seventeen-year-old son, Prince Ferdinand. Although Aragón was much smaller than Castile, it was important because the two kingdoms shared a border. Isabella saw the political benefits to be gained from this proposed marriage. As king and queen of a united Aragón and Castile, she and Ferdinand could create a single country dedicated to the glory of God and the Catholic Church.

Enrique and his supporters were against the marriage. They still wanted Isabella to marry King Afonso V of Portugal, a marriage which would take her far from Castile but would make it possible to unite Portugal and Castile under one crown. Isabella had rejected marriage to King

This map shows the kingdoms of Castile and Aragón in the fifteenth century.

Afonso once and was prepared to do so a second time. When she made this clear to Enrique, he was furious, but the teenage princess would not back down.

To test her political strength, Isabella decided to visit Avila, a town Enrique had awarded her by the Toros de Guisando. She expected a warm welcome from the citizens there, but to her surprise, she was turned away at the gate and told Enrique was their ruler. Enrique had double-crossed her. He had promised this town and others to her but had never intended to hand them over. In fact, Enrique was also planning to renounce Isabella's claim to the throne and to name La Beltraneja as his heir.

2

Lies and Betrayals

Eighteen-year-old Isabella was in a dangerous predica-
ment. She knew Enrique had lied to her, but if she con-
fronted him she risked being imprisoned or killed. First she
needed to find supporters—and to do so without his finding
out. Marriage to Ferdinand might be her only option. They
shared the same language and customs and were almost the
same age. They were also second cousins, and their union
would reconnect a dynasty that had begun five generations
before. Their marriage would unite a large part of the Iberian
Peninsulaunder the double crowns of Castile and Aragón.

Though Isabella had promised Enrique she would not
arrange a marriage without his permission, she turned to her
old friend Archbishop Carrillo. He was happy to negotiate
a secret marriage agreement with Aragón. Carrillo pointed
out that Enrique had already broken the treaty when he

reneged on his pledge to award the regions he had promised to Isabella—this freed her to break her promise to him.

The next weeks were a stressful period for Isabella. She had to pretend to be loyal to Enrique while her allies worked feverishly behind the scenes to arrange her marriage. Enrique suspected some kind of plot was in the works. He tried to find a way to marry Isabella off and have her sent far away from Castile. He also hinted in public that he planned to announce that La Beltraneja was his true heir. Isabella realized she needed to be married as soon as possible. Only with Ferdinand's support could she hope to become queen of Castile. She urged Carrillo to hurry.

Drafting a marriage agreement was not a simple matter. Carrillo, traveling under diplomatic pretexts to fool Enrique's spies, spent many hours with representatives of Aragón hammering out the details. Isabella was the heir to a large and powerful kingdom, and Carrillo wanted to protect her interests—and his own. The marriage contract specified a separation of powers between the prince and princess that kept the kingdoms of Castile and Aragón mostly separate. While Ferdinand would inherit Aragón upon his father's death, most of his attention and obligations would focus on Castile. He would move there to live with Isabella, and when she became queen he would be crowned as her king consort. This would limit his powers. Isabella would make all municipal, civil, and religious appointments. Ferdinand would make military decisions as commander of the army and would wage war against any enemies of the Catholic faith. Although many royal decisions would be made mutually,

Prince Ferdinand of Aragón.

Isabella's decisions would take precedence over Ferdinand's if there was a dispute. Ferdinand would obey the laws of Castile and would appoint only Castilians to office.

Ferdinand signed the marriage agreement on January 7, 1469. With it came a letter from his bride-to-be. Isabella had to be circumspect in case her letter was intercepted and used against her, so she wrote a few simple sentences then signed it, meaningfully, "From the hand which will do whatever you command." Once the signed marriage contract was in her possession, Isabella wrote to Enrique to ask for his blessing. There was no reply. She also wrote to the pope, asking for a papal dispensation to allow her marriage, which was necessary because she and Ferdinand were second cousins. For his part, Archbishop Carrillo was traveling the countryside, polling the nobility to ensure Isabella's hasty marriage would meet with their approval. He knew they could not risk making an alliance without the support of the nobility.

While Isabella waited for news, Ferdinand was struggling with a decision of his own. He was aware of the need to finalize the marriage quickly. But he was chief military commander of Aragón, and his father had ordered him to mount a counter-offensive against invading French armies. Ferdinand had little formal schooling, but he had grown up on the battlefields. He had to decide to go back to the war or to leave his father, marry, and possibly gain a kingdom. Ferdinand chose to go to Isabella. Because he feared that military officers might try to force him to remain in Aragón or that Enrique's supporters might try to keep him away from Isabella, he disguised himself in ragged clothes and traveled to Castile by mule. Only a few companions accompanied him.

When Isabella heard Ferdinand was on his way to her, she wrote to Enrique again. Again, Enrique failed to answer. Isabella sent another letter telling him that she was of sufficient age and maturity to make her own marriage decisions and asked him to bless her choice. He did not. Isabella knew for certain now that Enrique was going to renounce her in favor of La Beltraneja.

In October 1469, Isabella and Ferdinand finally came face to face in the middle of the night. Eighteen-year-old Isabella was plump and attractive. Seventeen-year-old

The betrothal of Isabella and Ferdinand.

Ferdinand was of medium height with dark brown eyes and hair. He was dressed in coarse clothing and had traveled most of a day and night to reach her. He brought as a gift for his future bride an enormous ruby and pearl necklace. The two had little time to speak, but an immediate spark of attraction passed between them.

On October 18, Archbishop Carrillo presented the dispensation from the pope. Isabella and Ferdinand were married the next day. Soon afterwards, they wrote to King Enrique, asking to be excused for not waiting for his permission to marry and declaring that they hoped to bring harmony and peace to Castile. They explained that their

Isabella and Ferdinand's coat of arms.

haste in sealing the union was necessary in order to have children right away to insure there was a line of succession to the throne. They were trying to give Enrique a way to approve their marriage without losing face, but they received no answer.

Once the excitement of their marriage had passed, Ferdinand and Isabella had time to get to know one another. They discovered that they had many mutual interests. Both attended Mass daily, were skilled riders, and enjoyed games of chess and cards. Both were disciplined and orderly. Most importantly, both were determined to become king and queen of a united Castile and Aragón. Following tradition, they chose symbols for their coat of arms: Isabella chose arrows, or *flechas,* for the first letter of Ferdinand's name, and he chose a yoke, or *yugo*, for the Y or I of Isabella. The arrows, yoke, and the symbols of Castile, León, and Aragón were made into a new coat of arms, completed by the Gordian knot, the symbol of everlasting love. The couple dispatched letters throughout the kingdoms proclaiming that Aragón and Castile were united for the glory of the Catholic faith.

A few weeks later, Ferdinand and Isabella learned why Enrique had not answered their many requests for a blessing of the marriage. He waited until they settled down into domestic life and then announced publicly that they were living in sin. He claimed the pope had not issued the required dispensation for their marriage. When questioned, Archbishop Carrillo admitted he had forged the paper. His excuse was that the political situation would not allow a delay and that he knew the actual dispensation would arrive any day. Isabella was horrified and believed that both she and Ferdinand were condemned to the eternal fires of hell. They sent an emergency messenger to Pope Paul II in Rome asking for an immediate dispensation.

Isabella did not sit idly by and wait for the answer. She visited an emissary of the pope and proposed a secret bargain in return for a speedy dispensation. If she received it quickly, she and Ferdinand promised to send money to help the pope in his attempts to stop the Ottoman Turks from expanding further into Europe. She was still awaiting a reply in 1470 when she gave birth to a daughter who was christened Isabel. The couple was disappointed their first child was not a boy. Having a male heir would solidify Isabella's claim to the throne of Castile and insure that Ferdinand had an heir for Aragón. Aragón, unlike Castile, followed the tradition of Salic Law, which meant the throne could be passed only from one male member of the family to another.

Enrique took advantage of Isabel's birth to try to strengthen La Beltraneja's claim to the throne. He announced that he was canceling all of his promises to Isabella as punishment for disobeying him by marrying Ferdinand. Because of Isabella's illegal and sacrilegious actions, he said, she was not an appropriate candidate for the throne. He declared that La Beltraneja was his true heir.

This act officially disinherited Isabella. But neither she nor Ferdinand, nor their constituents, accepted the disinheritance. Isabella, Ferdinand, and their baby were popular figures. They were devout, modest, and forthright. Enrique, by contrast, was weak and untrustworthy. Most people believed La Beltraneja was not his daughter and were tired of his rule. Isabella then made a bold move. She wrote to Enrique and warned him that if he continued to question her right to the throne, he would only be providing impetus for a rebellion that would remove him from power: "God will make you . . . responsible for such a great evil, while my Lord, the Prince and I and the ones who follow . . . will be free of all blame."

Isabella was gambling that the people of Castile would see her as a strong leader who was determined to end the corruption and immorality that characterized Enrique's reign. Isabella and Ferdinand traveled from town to town in Castile to make themselves known and to gain support. They promised to bring reform to the kingdom. Their popularity

Isabella, Ferdinand, and their daughter Isabel are shown here praying to the Virgin Mary. *(The Prado Museum, Madrid)*

deepened and widened; anti-Enrique rebels grew in number and strength.

One of the enduring characteristics of Isabella's rule would be the combination of determination and shrewdness she brought to the throne. She realized that gaining political support was a matter of winning minds, but that gaining popular support was a matter of gaining hearts. Isabella was aware of the importance of her personal charisma and the necessity of looking like a queen. In public appearances she wore sumptuous satins and velvets adorned with sparkling jewels. Ferdinand dressed in long robes or knee-length vests of silk and velvet, sometimes trimmed with embroidery, sometimes with fur. He wore thick gold necklaces and perfumed gloves. Though Isabella was very devout, the only way she ever signified her love of worldly goods was in the jewels and clothing she wore—including Ferdinand's gift to her, that tremendous ruby and pearl necklace. Isabella backed up her royal appearance with strong words, openly condemning Enrique. She was willing to stake her life on the belief that the citizens of Castile were tired of his rule.

3

Crowning a Queen

Castile was the largest kingdom on the Iberian Peninsula, a region bordered by the Atlantic Ocean on the west and the Mediterranean Sea on the south. A few dusty highways connected the Castilian cities, villages, and walled towns of straw-thatched huts and whitewashed stucco homes. Nearly every town had its own church and a public well. Beyond the city gates were great tracts of farmlands, owned by the wealthy *grandees* and the church. The towns had little connection with each other or to the larger cities. News traveled slowly, carried from town to town by peddlers and royal courtiers. Aragón was a smaller kingdom to the east. The kingdom of Portugal stretched along the western edge of the peninsula, a long, narrow piece of land with hundreds of miles of border on the Atlantic Ocean.

Castile had been through a series of succession crises

A typical Castilian town in the fifteenth century.

over the previous two hundred years. Although none had reached the level of tension that existed between Enrique and Isabella, there had been many skirmishes. Most nobles maintained private armies that they commanded as they saw fit. The high walls built around towns were there to protect citizens from the lawlessness that ruled the countryside.

Most of the region's climate was dry and dusty. The only consistently fertile area was in Andalusia, to the south. The people of the Iberian Peninsula were accustomed to famines. Frequent outbreaks of the Black Death caused further pain and suffering.

Conflict over royal succession was not the only political issue dividing the peninsula. Religion was another major problem. During the eighth century, the southern part of the peninsula had been invaded and conquered by Muslims from North Africa. After seizing control, the Muslims, who were called Moors, built grand mosques, government buildings, and towers with porticoed arches and walls made of stucco, a combination of cement, sand, and lime. Many of their structures were accented with beautiful woodcarvings, mosaics, and tiles. The Moors had also maintained, and added to, many of the intellectual advances of the classical era while Europe's thinking had languished during the Middle Ages—nearly a thousand years. The Moors brought with them this legacy of learning including advanced studies in medicine, mathematics, philosophy, and literature.

ISLAMIC SPAIN

When Muhammad, the prophet of Islam, died in 632, he had converted most of the Arabian Peninsula to the new, monotheistic faith. His successors were determined to spread Muhammad's message throughout the world and soon began a series of military conquests. Before the decade was out, the Muslims, as the practitioners of Islam were called, had conquered most of the Mediterranean coast and moved east into Persia. Almost simultaneously, they began to spread steadily west across Northern

Africa. Egypt fell in 646, and by the end of the century, all of Northern Africa had converted to Islam.

The Muslims brought more than a new religion to the areas that they controlled. Although

This ancient miniature shows the prophet Muhammad with some of his followers.

Muhammad was illiterate, as were many of his original followers, the spread of Islam brought Muslims in contact with societies, such as the Egyptians, that had long traditions of literacy. As Islam became more organized, literacy spread, so that by the end of the seventh century, Arabic, the language of the Koran, had spread throughout the Middle East and Northern Africa. There were also dramatic increases in literacy and the development of educationl systems. Universities and other schools flourished in the Islamic world.

Muslims invaded Spain in 711, and by 719 they dominated the area between the Strait of Gibraltar and the Pyrenees Mountains. During these years of conquest there was also a great deal of turmoil over control of the faith. This resulted in the historical split between the Sunni and the Shia sects, which continues to this day. The Umayyad dynasty, which controlled Islam until around 750, was established in Damascus. For the first time, the center of the faith was not on the Arabian Peninsula. The Umayyad were succeeded by the Abbâsids, whose rule lasted until 1258.

At the time of the Islamic conquest, Spain was made up of a variety of peoples, including Berbers from Northern Africa, Celts from Europe, and Visigoths from Central Asia. The Muslims defeated Roderick, the last of the Visigoth kings, at the Battle of Rio Barbate. The Muslim invasion continued north until it was stopped by the Frankish ruler Charles Martel in 732. Only a small section of northern Spain remained Christian by the end of the eighth century.

By the ninth century, Islamic Spain was the wonder of Europe. The capital city of Córdoba had become the intellectual center of the continent. The city had over five hundred thousand inhabitants. There were over seven hundred mosques, and the beautiful Arabic style houses had marble balconies and impressive gardens. There were publishers, a thriving literature, libraries, and public gardens. In the outlying areas, irrigation systems had turned the dry plains green and several crops imported from the Middle East, including pomegranates, lemons, and almonds, were grown for export.

Students came from all over Europe to study in Córdoba, where

This minaret, a classic example of Moorish architecture, is part of the mosque in the city of Seville in southern Spain.

Jewish, Muslim, and Christian scholars researched and taught side by side. There was a level of religious tolerance in the city that was impossible in the rest of Europe. The focus on secular learning and economic prosperity made it easier for people of differing faiths to live with relatively little conflict. The only penalty for being a non-Muslim was the payment of an extra tax.

This period of prosperity and cultural development eventually fell victim to a series of internal struggles between warring factions and invasions from antagonistic Arab forces. The great library in Córdoba was destroyed in 1013. The internal strife provided an opportunity for the Christians to the north to organize a series of invasions that began the process of driving the Muslims from Spain. Paradoxically, it was the European plunder of the cultural treasures of Islamic Spain that might have provided the final impetus for the development of the Renaissance in Italy and elsewhere. Many of the works of classical antiquity, including works on astronomy, mathematics, medicine, philosophy, and history, first entered Europe as Latin translations of Arabic books.

While the Christian reconquest of Spain preserved a great deal of the Islamic intellectual and cultural achievements, much of the architecture and other public works were destroyed.

The derivation of the word Moors, which was used generally to refer to Islamic culture on the Iberian Peninsula and the people from Northern Africa who crossed the strait into Spain, is somewhat ambiguous, and the term is not used as frequently today as in the past.

Between the eighth and fifteenth centuries, the Moors and the Christians had fought many battles and territory had been gained and lost. Over the last two hundred years, the tide had slowly shifted in the favor of the Christians. By the 1400s, Christians controlled most of the Iberian Peninsula, except for Granada in southern Spain, which was still a predominantly Muslim enclave. A tentative peace agreement had been reached, but lingering resentment and animosity, strengthened by the religious and cultural differences, still simmered between the Christians and the Moors. In Castile, the term "good citizen" came to mean more than a responsible law-abiding person; it also meant a deeply religious Catholic who served both God and his country.

The Catholic Church was an extremely powerful force in much of Europe in the fifteenth century. Church officials were not only exempt from paying taxes but also had the power to levy taxes on cities and villages, nobles, businessmen, traders, and farmers. It was a power they did not hesitate to use. As a result, the church had a good deal of money, as did individual members of the clergy. Castile had over fifty bishops at any given time, and many of the holders of this powerful office had large estates and private armies. The power of the church rivaled or surpassed that of any secular ruler.

The Catholic Church was centered in far away Rome. From there, the pope, who Catholics considered to be divinely appointed by God, dictated church policies and procedures. Increasingly, he was pressuring Christian rulers in Iberia and other European regions to convert Jews and other non-Christians. There had been conflict between Christians and Jews all over Europe during the fourteenth and fifteenth centuries. During the horrible Black Death of 1348-51, when the bubonic plague killed a third of Europe's population, some blamed it on the Jews, charging that they had poisoned the wells. Others believed the plague was a punishment from God for allowing Jewish people to live with Christians. When it was discovered that the plague was probably spread by rats, it was said that migrating Jews had brought the rats to Europe. Mobs of Christians persecuted Jews, subjecting them to torture, exile, and murder.

Oddly enough, the Catholic Church was partly responsible for the Jews initially being welcomed into Spain and other European countries. The church forbade its followers to engage in usury (charging interest on loans). Because Jews were not bound by such restrictions they were able to serve a necessary purpose in Spanish society, which soon had the largest Jewish population in Europe. Access to capital was critical to maintain the flourishing trade that passed through the peninsula. However, one effect of this reliance on money-lending was that it enriched some members of the Jewish population. This made many Christians jealous and angry. In 1391, one rabble-rousing preacher brought anti-Jewish sentiment to such a fevered pitch that approximately four thousand Jews were killed in the city of Seville alone. Pogroms against the Jews continued, with varying levels of intensity, over the following decades.

It has been estimated that the pogroms of 1391 resulted in the deaths of approximately one hundred thousand Jews, the exile of another hundred thousand, and the conversion to Christianity of a hundred thousand more. Those that converted were made to confess their sins, undergo baptism, and attend mass. Some of the new Christians, or *conversos*, took their conversions seriously and became believers in Christianity. Others only pretended to convert to avoid persecution and secretly did their best to stay true to their Jewish faith. They washed the holy oils from their infants' bodies as soon as possible after baptism, invited rabbis to their homes for secret instruction, and ate pork (forbidden by Judaaism) only when there was no way to avoid it.

Conversos occupied a difficult place in society. While they were more accepted than those who continued to openly practice Judaism, many Christians doubted their sincerity. *Conversos* often endured the same indignities and insults as the unconverted. As years went by, the following generations were still considered *conversos* even if they knew nothing at all about their ancestors' faith. Religious tensions were always high, but the pogroms of 1391 brought them to the boiling point.

While *conversos* were discriminated against, those who remained true to the Jewish faith were treated even more poorly. In 1412, their outsider status was codified into law. Jews were specifically barred from a number of occupations, from employing Christians, and from holding public office. They were also forced to identify themselves by wearing their hair long and following a proscribed style of dress.

Tenuous relations between Christians, *conversos*, and Jews were again upset during Lent of 1473. In Córdoba, a maid dumped the contents of a pot out of a window, inadvertently splashing a statue of the Virgin Mary that was being carried through the streets. Word quickly spread that the liquid, which might have been water, was actually urine. Enraged Catholics gathered outside the house, which happened to belong to a *converso* family. Though the maid protested her innocence, the alleged insult brought the whole city into the streets. Within hours, Christians were shouting "We are going to avenge ourselves for this great injury and everyone will die who are traitors and heretics!" and "Death to the *conversos*!"

For three days, rioters burned and rampaged through the city, into the suburbs, and out to neighboring towns. In one town after another, Spanish inhabitants assaulted Jews, releasing years of pent-up violence and hatred.

Enrique's tenuous hold over his kingdom was further threatened by this increase in violence and other lawlessness. His split with Isabella was costing him support.

Now that she had started to speak against him publicly, Enrique knew it was only a matter of time before there was bloodshed. He decided to act. One winter day, an old peasant woman arrived at Isabella's palace. Isabella soon discovered that she was a member of Enrique's court in disguise, named Beatriz de Bobadilla, who had come at the king's request.

A Jewish man in the required dress, from an engraving by Jean-Baptiste Van Mour. *(The Israel Museum, Jerusalem)*

Enrique wanted to meet secretly with his half-sister to try to reconcile their differences. Isabella debated what to do. She did not trust Enrique; he had broken too many promises. But she risked damaging her reputation if word got out that she had refused to accept his offer to negotiate. She knew that reconciliation would be good for her country. Enrique wanted her to bring little Isabel to Segovia as evidence of her good faith. Though it was common for children to be used as collateral, or hostages, while negotiating treaties, Isabella rejected this request. She remembered all too well being separated from her own mother when she was forced to live in Enrique's court. Enrique finally dropped the condition and she agreed to the meeting.

On December 28, 1473, Enrique and Isabella met in Segovia. The atmosphere was warm and cordial; brother and sister seemed genuinely glad to see each other. They had both changed since their last meeting. Twenty-two-year-old Isabella was more confident and determined. Forty-nine-year-old Enrique was recovering from a recent illness and showing the effects of nearly twenty years of difficult rule and unhealthy living. The king was tired; he knew his grip on the country was faltering.

Isabella opened the meeting. She wanted to ensure that Enrique honored their blood relationship and that he would affirm that Isabella was the legitimate successor to his throne. Enrique listened impassively. The next day the pair appeared at a magnificent feast, complete with white linen tablecloths, tureens of boar and venison, and musicians with stringed instruments. There was no talk of succession. The day after, Isabella and Enrique went out in public. She rode through the streets of Segovia on a white horse while Enrique walked alongside her holding the reins. Segovians lined the streets and watched, silently approving what seemed to be a reconciliation. But still, Enrique refused to discuss the matter of succession to the crown.

Enrique invited Ferdinand to join the festivities, and he arrived on New Year's Day, 1474. A feast that began in the early afternoon continued until candles were lit. Isabella's advisors had warned against meeting with Enrique. They worried he was planning to arrest her or kidnap her daughter—or worse. But Isabella would not be dissuaded. She believed Enrique could be convinced to do what was right.

By January 9, the atmosphere in Segovia was still warm and friendly. Guests feasted on an enormous meal and then were offered a huge table of puff pastries, cheese tarts, and other desserts. Enrique and Isabella were enjoying the food when, suddenly, he doubled over in pain and had to be helped to the royal bedchamber. Doctors were summoned, and rumors that the king had been poisoned ran rampant.

The next day all the priests, monks, and nuns of Segovia prayed. Citizens lined the streets in a vigil. Isabella and Ferdinand stayed as close to Enrique as they could. He seemed to recover for a few days, but then relapsed. His most visible symptoms were diarrhea and bloody urine. Isabel and Ferdinand knew that they should speak with him about succession as soon as he seemed ready to talk, but Enrique and his aides brushed them away whenever they tried to open the discussion. Then, one morning in March, Enrique was nowhere to be found. In the middle of the night he had left Segovia.

Isabella stayed behind, waiting for news. Time dragged on as spring became summer became fall. The couple decided that Ferdinand could leave Segovia to help his father fight the French. Finally, in December of 1474, word reached Isabella that Enrique was dying. As he lay on his deathbed, his ministers begged him to name an heir to the

The city of Segovia, where Isabella met with Enrique and where she was eventually crowned queen of Castile.

throne. Would it be the twelve-year-old La Beltraneja or his half-sister Isabella? Enrique would not answer. He died on December 12, still refusing to name an heir. Even before Enrique's body was cold, Isabella's supporters in his court sent her a messenger. He rode through the night and arrived at Segovia less than twenty-four hours later.

Her allies and counselors advised Isabella to take the throne immediately, before La Beltraneja and her supporters could mount their own campaign. She would have liked Ferdinand to be there at her coronation so he could be officially named king consort, but dared not wait. In her heart, Isabella felt justified in accepting the throne because Enrique had formally named her heir in 1469. Although he had later retracted the promise, most Castilians believed it could not be retracted legally.

On the morning of December 13, 1474, around twenty-four hours after the death of Enrique, Isabella dressed in dark mourning clothes and attended a funeral mass for her half-brother. Then she returned to the castle and changed

Isabella's coronation at the Church of San Miguel in Segovia.

into an elegant jewel-trimmed gown. She donned necklaces
and bracelets trimmed with pearls and other gems, including the famous ruby and pearl necklace Ferdinand had given

her. All over Segovia, people poured into the streets to see their new queen. People of all classes came to pay their respects—blacksmiths, tanners, tonsured monks, mothers with their children, millers, and shepherds. Nobles gathered silently around the castle entrance dressed in their best winter finery. When twenty-three-year-old Isabella emerged, she mounted a horse decorated in beautiful livery. City officials raised a brocade canopy over her head.

Isabella led a procession through the streets, ending at a platform that had been hastily erected in the town square. A fanfare of trumpets and horns sounded, then a herald cried "Castile, Castile, for the Queen and our Proprietress the Queen Doña Isabella and for the King Don Ferdinand, her legitimate husband!" Church bells rang and cannons boomed as Isabella's old ally, Carrillo, the archbishop of Toledo, placed a silver crown on her head. Each of the nobles present came forward to swear allegiance to the new queen.

Isabella led the procession to the Church of San Miguel where she and her court sang hymns of praise. The audience of papal ambassadors, knights, nobles, priests, and towns-people cheered as she put her right hand on the Bible and swore to uphold the commandments of the Catholic Church. Then, at the altar, she prayed to God for strength and wisdom. For the ceremonies that followed, Isabella followed behind a single horseman who carried a sword pointing at the sky. Never before had the sword been raised for a woman crowned alone, but Isabella was determined to show her new subjects that she was no ordinary ruler. She was resolved to uphold justice and restore Castile to honor.

One of Isabella's first actions as queen was to write to the cities and towns of the realm, asking them to acknowledge her ascension to the throne and to swear their loyalty to the new monarchs. She knew it was critical that she and Ferdinand quickly get the recognition and support of the nobility and cities.

The newly crowned King Ferdinand.

Ferdinand received the news of Enrique's death three days after the fact. He was stunned to hear that the coronation of his wife had taken place without his presence. Realizing he would be upset, Isabella asked him to delay his return to Segovia for a few days. She wanted to prepare a welcome worthy of him. When Ferdinand arrived on January 2, 1475, he was met at the gates by clergy and townspeople bearing crosses. Looking kingly and proud in his flowing fur coat, he was asked one question: Would he reign with Isabella? He answered yes. The councilmen then swore to "obey and receive His Highness as legitimate husband of Our Lady the Queen for their King and Lord."

One of the lessons Isabella had learned from Enrique's

Queen Isabella and King Ferdinand. *(University of Valladolid Library)*

failed reign was the importance of ceremony. Enrique had shunned it, but Isabella understood the power of symbolism. She made a point to dress in rich, elaborate clothes and to infuse public ceremonies with dignity and grace. When Ferdinand arrived in Segovia she welcomed him in a public reception. Their first meeting as king and queen revealed the new monarchs to be modest, devout, devoted to each other, and regal. Isabella and Ferdinand showed their subjects they were rulers to be respected and admired.

Privately, however, Ferdinand and Isabella quarreled. He resented that she had been crowned without him, and that he was merely her king consort, not king in his own right. He particularly objected to Isabella's announcement that upon her death the throne would go to their daughter Isabel and not to him. Isabella replied that these decisions were not hers, but were prescribed by custom, tradition, and the terms of their marriage agreement. Ferdinand could never be ruler of Castile because he was not a direct descendant of the original ruling family. Still, Ferdinand protested.

The couple finally agreed to have their disagreement decided by a council of legal experts. Female succession was unusual in those times, but Isabella's talent for logical reasoning convinced the council that she was right. She told Ferdinand that "this subject [succession], Lord, need never to have been discussed because where there is such union as by the grace of God exists between you and me, there can be no difference. Already, as my husband, you are King of Castile." Isabella further reminded the group that if Isabel inherited the throne, she would doubtless marry a royal from another country and the only way to protect Castile from that prince's rule would be to ensure Isabel was its queen. In the end, the council agreed.

Isabella's level head and willingness to speak her mind in a roomful of men demonstrated to her subjects that she was a strong queen. To keep Ferdinand from being relegated to the shadows, the royal couple adopted the motto *Tanto Monta, Monta Tanto,* or "One is equal to the other." Over the years, Isabella gave Ferdinand more power and responsibility. One of the great strengths of their rule was the strong foundation laid by their marriage. Each was the other's most respected advisor as they worked together to make their kingdom strong.

4

Uniting Spain

The first challenge Isabella and Ferdinand faced was to show the nobility that they were in control. Weak kings had ruled Castile for so long that much of the power had drifted into the hands of the wealthy and landed nobility. This led to a kingdom that was often divided between warring families, each with its own army. It was left up to the isolated towns and cities to provide protection for their own citizens. The result was a decentralized government lacking a strong ruler.

The situation was made more complicated because Enrique's putative daughter, La Beltraneja, had also claimed the throne. Her supporters tried to arrange her marriage to Afonso V, the king of Portugal, in order to use Portugal's might to claim Castile. It would take five years for Isabella and Ferdinand to eliminate La Beltraneja as a contender.

These tensions highlighted the problems that Enrique's weak government had created. Under Enrique, *grandees* had been allowed to acquire great wealth at the expense of the lower classes. The judicial system favored the wealthy, and the masses had nowhere to go with their complaints. The treasury was depleted because of Enrique's efforts to

Isabella's rival for the throne, Juana La Beltraneja.

buy the support of the *grandees*. Many citizens had lived under corrupt government for so long that they were suspicious of any authority. Isabella met resistance to her efforts to create a strong central government. Neither the *grandees* nor the church wanted to relinquish their power. Her faith helped to keep her steadfast in the face of opposition. She often prayed: "My Lord Jesus Christ, I leave everything in your hands and I expect to be defended by your favor and help."

Organizing the kingdom was going to be a major project. In order to work as effectively and quickly as possible, the

The walled city of Trujillo, in Spain's Extremadura region, still stands today.

royal couple split up. Ferdinand traveled north to quell rebellions. Isabella traveled west to Extremadura, a region on the Portuguese border, to do the same.

Isabella's first stop was the city of Trujillo. Twice, the mayor of the city refused her entrance, until Isabella gathered a small army behind her and approached the city gates on horseback. "I will enter my city understanding that it is mine through God's service," she announced. Cowed, the mayor opened the gates and order was restored.

The new queen effected a similar change in the neighboring city of Cáceres. Isabella encountered no resistance when she entered the city, but she was angry that its citizens had not supported her in the past. Taking a hard line, she ordered that rebel leaders be hanged and their homes torn down. She announced the end of elections for public officials and said that from that time on she would appoint all leaders. Her pronouncements met with little protest. Though Isabella's rule was harsh, citizens seemed to prefer it to the weak leadership of Enrique.

Once Ferdinand and Isabella had gathered their kingdom under their rule, they were able to look beyond their own lands. Until the fifteenth century, the regions that make up present day Spain had not often participated in European affairs. None of the kingdoms was powerful enough to pursue a foreign policy, and generations of warring factions had kept them divided. Because their marriage united the two most powerful states, Castile and Aragón, Isabella and Ferdinand could now dream of a united Spain that would be of international importance. Before this united Spain could become a reality, however, much still had to be done. The French continued to press over the northern border near the Pyrenees Mountains. On the western border, King Afonso of Portugal still dreamed of adding Aragón and Castile to his kingdom by marrying La Beltraneja and then challenging Isabella and Ferdinand. Portugal was also geographically important. Not only did it border Castile but its long coastline was a rich source for fish and, more importantly, provided access to valuable sea routes that could be used for commerce in gold and slaves from West Africa.

Ferdinand and Isabella had to first build loyalty within their own borders. They held magnificent pageants and sporting exhibitions where contestants and participants dressed in glittering armor and elegant costumes. Isabella appeared in grand outfits, often astride a white horse harnessed in silver and covered with golden flowers. They opened their family activities to many of their staff—lawyers and judges, security guards, chefs and stewards, and personal valets—people who were not *grandees.* Although these entertainments were not inexpensive, they helped to secure political loyalty.

The next challenge for the royals was to win the support of the *cortes,* a legislative body made up of representatives from all the cities and towns of the kingdom. There was no rule regulating how often a *cortes* would meet. Monarchs traditionally summoned a *cortes* when they needed money and wanted the *cortes* to impose taxes, or needed support for the military or for diplomatic matters, such as the arranged marriages of their children. Assembling the *cortes* could provide political cover for a ruler because it allowed him to share responsibility for decisions. But it could also be risky. Unfortunately for Ferdinand and Isabella, when they called the *cortes,* many cities did not send representatives, thereby implying their loyalty was to no one—or to La Beltraneja. Without a unified *cortes,* the other members refused to give the royals the money they requested. Ferdinand and Isabella were broke. This meant that as the royal couple continued the arduous process of bringing order to their kingdom they had to rely heavily on the nobles still loyal to the crown for financial and military support.

They also had to worry about the possibility of war with Portugal. Afonso was massing troops along the border. Then the dreaded news arrived. Afonso sent a message to Ferdinand and Isabella that he and La Beltraneja were betrothed, and that after the wedding, they would claim the throne of

Castile. Isabella replied that La Beltraneja had no claim to the throne. Afonso responded by sending gifts to Castilian knights in an effort to win them over to his side. He also accused Isabella and Ferdinand of ruining Castile's economy, poisoning King Enrique, and illegally seizing the throne.

Isabella and Ferdinand both exerted tremendous effort to visit their troops in battle in order to both raise morale and personally inspect their condition.

By the summer of 1475, Portugal and Castile were officially at war. The royal couple worked feverishly to raise money and troops. Ferdinand traveled to neighboring regions to ask for their support and to recruit and train soldiers. Isabella shrewdly sent out proclamations saying she would pardon all rebels who abandoned Portugal and came to the aid of Castile. She devoted herself to the war effort around the clock, writing letters, issuing orders, raising money, even riding from town to town asking for support. An accomplished horsewoman, Isabella exhausted the fastest horses racing over the countryside. One of these rides might have cost her and Ferdinand a son—Isabella miscarried a baby boy that summer.

The royal couple was seldom together. Ferdinand learned of the miscarriage in a letter. Both he and Isabella mourned the loss; only a son could guarantee Aragón and Castile would remain united at their deaths. In addition to the strain of losing the baby, Isabella and Ferdinand disagreed over whether she should try to reconcile with her old supporter Archbishop Carrillo. He had abandoned their cause for Portugal's because he felt Isabella had not adequately rewarded him for his devoted service. Isabella had never forgiven him for forging the papal dispensation. Now Isabella wanted to try to convince him to give up his support for Afonso. Ferdinand disagreed with this decision and Isabella resented Ferdinand's lack of support for her actions. She even cut off communication with him for a time.

When days had passed without mail from Isabella, Ferdinand wrote to her: "The reason why you do not write is not because there is no paper to be had, or that you do not know how to write, but because you do not love me and because you are proud." Isabella did not respond. Both she and her husband had stubborn personalities. It was only their mutual faith in God and devotion to their kingdom that kept them from splintering apart.

Isabella and Ferdinand amassed 42,000 men to defend their territory. Although this was a fair-sized army, the fighters were undisciplined, poorly equipped, and underfed. They suffered in the sweltering heat. After one ignominious defeat, Isabella met them as they retreated from the town of Toro. She harangued them for running from the battle and warned them, "If you say to me that women, since they do not face such dangers, ought not to speak of them . . . to this I say that I do not know who risks more than I do, for I risked my King and Lord . . . and so many men and riches. . . . I would wish to pursue uncertain danger rather than certain shame." She insisted that they return to the battlefield.

She vented her anger at Ferdinand as well: "If you had forced the forts open, and I don't doubt that you would if you had my will, Portugal and its sovereignty would have been lost in memory." Ferdinand retorted: "I thought that coming back defeated I would find words of consolation and encouragement from your mouth but you complain because we have returned whole and with no glory lost? Well, we will certainly have a heavy task to satisfy you from here on! . . . Women are always malcontent, and you especially, My Lady, since the man who could satisfy you is yet to be born."

This argument, however, marked a turning point for the couple. Each realized the other needed unquestioning support, not condemnation and blame. They could triumph only if they worked together. From that time on, Isabella served as Ferdinand's quartermaster, supplying his troops from behind the lines and ensuring that he had everything he needed to succeed. Working together, they marshaled their paltry resources more effectively and managed to hold off Afonso's troops for several years. Finally, Afonso suggested a settlement. He agreed to give up his claim to the Castilian crown in return for the Castilian province of Galicia, the cities of Toro and Zamora, and a large sum of money. Isabella's answer was quick and defiant. She would not cede one inch of Castilian land.

The conflict was going to continue, and the situation was growing desperate. Money was the greatest obstacle. The loyal nobles had given her all they could and the *cortes* still refused to vote any additional funds. She had only one option left. Isabella turned to the church, arguing that the interests of Castile were identical to the interests of the Catholic Church. The church agreed to loan her an amount equal to one half of its resources. With new funding, Isabella was finally able to soundly defeat the Portuguese at Burgos, near the northern border of Castile. A little more than a month later, twenty-four-year-old Isabella waded through knee-deep snowdrifts in a blizzard to preside over the Portuguese surrender at Burgos. The war was not over, but the tide had turned. Portugal no longer held the upper hand.

In August 1476, aides awakened Isabella with the word that five-year-old Isabel, who was staying in Segovia, might be in danger. Citizens were rebelling against the rule of *converso* Governor Andres de Cabrera, whom they accused of being too strict. Isabella immediately called for her horse and began an arduous twenty-four-hour ride over difficult terrain. When she reached the city gates, Governor Cabrera's supporters warned her there would be violence if she entered. Isabella answered, "I am queen of Castile and this city is mine."

Isabella and her entourage proceeded unharmed through the winding streets to the town square. There she faced the gathering crowds and asked what their grievances were. Stunned by her question, the people managed to say that they were unhappy with Cabrera's harsh rule. Surprising the crowd further, she promised to remove him from office until a hearing about the matter could be held. Isabella's cool and rational approach to the problem deflated much of the crowd's anger. Little Isabel was reunited with her mother. Crowds followed her through the streets shouting, "Long live the Queen!"

True to her word, Isabella arranged a public hearing. After listening carefully to testimony, she told the gathered citizens that she had determined that the Segovians had suffered from abuse by their officials, but not specifically from Cabrera. Accordingly, the corrupt officials would be removed and Cabrera reinstated. The citizens assented without protest—the queen had won their confidence.

Realizing that other cities faced similar problems, Isabella and Ferdinand called the *cortes* together again and set about establishing the framework for a centralized government. They invited the seventeen municipalities in Castile to send petitions to the crown when they had grievances to be addressed. They discontinued the practice of giving government positions as favors and rewards. They insisted that local officials be promoted based on ability instead. To create financial stability, Isabella and Ferdinand standardized Castilian coins and restricted the amount of interest that moneylenders could charge.

The judicial system was overhauled. Trials were speeded up and the accused were provided with lawyers to plead their cases. They imposed drastic punishments on criminals, ranging from being beaten to being tied to a post and shot at with arrows. They instituted a civilian police force, the

Santa Hermandad, or Holy Brotherhood. This force was not a new idea in Castile. The first *hermandad* was established in the twelfth century to deter violent crimes. Since then, the role of the *hermandad* had been determined by each ruler. Ferdinand and Isabella required that every hundred households join together and hire a *hermandad* policeman who was expected to apprehend anyone who committed robbery, murder, rape, or rebellion. The punishment for a serious crime was usually death. The *hermandad* was so successful that in just three years the crime rate was reduced to almost nothing. For the first time, Castilians were a disciplined population. However, the *hermandad* left a legacy of cruel and sadistic punishment. Order was achieved, but at a great cost.

Isabella and Ferdinand were intent on creating a unified Catholic identity for their kingdom. Having a police force helped to keep order, but they believed that only a common religion would truly bind the population together. When Isabella spoke of the future, she usually added "with the help of our Lord." Ferdinand and Isabella were able to create a strong consensus among their subjects that the king and queen had been chosen by God to restore honor and glory to Castile. Some even thought that Isabella was an embodiment of Christianity, miraculously brilliant and charismatic, perhaps even the second Virgin Mary.

Isabella surrounded herself with devoutly religious figures. Her court was a marked opposite of Enrique's. Instead of parties and drinking and card games there was quiet talk and prayer. Intent on keeping herself close to God, Isabella asked Father Hernando de Talavera to become her personal confessor. Talavera was renowned for his discipline and devotion. In an era where many Church officials believed they were entitled to riches and finery, Talavera remained committed to his oath of poverty and piety. He wore a hair shirt—an uncomfortable garment made of coarse goat

Isabella's spiritual advisor, Hernando de Talavera.

hair that was considered a way to show one's devotion to God and abstention from sin—and slept on a board. At their first meeting, Isabella knelt to confess. When Talavera remained seated, she told him that it was appropriate for both parties to kneel. Talavera answered that he was God's tribunal, and it was appropriate that Isabella kneel while he remained seated.

Isabella believed Talavera was exactly who she needed to help her guard against corruption and vice. She wrote to him, "May you give me intelligence and strength so that, with the help of your arm, I can pursue and achieve my charge, and bring peace in these kingdoms." Talavera responded that her request was undoubtedly inspired by a divine light, and that he had full confidence in her success both politically and religiously if she continued in her quest for communion with the church: "Renew through God your noble spirit and gain perfection." He urged her to become a model for her subjects in her service to God. In the coming years, Talavera would repeatedly chastise Isabella for the fine clothes she wore and the sumptuous food she served to guests. Isabella defended her actions as necessary for a queen to inspire faith and awe, but she would always be grateful for his help in staying close to God.

The war with Portugal dragged on. Isabella and Ferdinand took advantage of Castile's strong navy to antagonize Portugal abroad. They sent ships to Cape Verde, a group of Portuguese islands in the Atlantic Ocean four hundred miles west of Africa, to seize a base for expansion to Africa and to distract Afonso from his battles on the Iberian Peninsula. Isabella authorized her ships to raid Portuguese ports as they traveled. She also claimed control of the Canary Islands, a group of islands off the northwest coast of Africa. She insisted they had been part of her father's kingdom. The islands provided critical access to West Africa, a source of wheat and slaves.

The Canary Islands became even more important when bad weather in Castile ruined the area's wheat harvest and caused widespread famine. People were starving all across the countryside. Isabella banned almost all exports of wheat until the crisis was over. An exception to the ban was the

Isabella used the fearsome Castilian navy to fight Portugal and control much of Spain's Atlantic trade. Spain's navy made the country one of the most powerful in Europe until the famed defeat of the Spanish armada by England in 1588. *(Courtesy of Art Resource.)*

shipment of wheat to the Vatican. Thirteenth-century theologian Thomas Aquinas had decreed that communion wafers be made from wheat, and by providing wheat to the church, Isabella hoped to curry the pope's favor. She planned to ask him to declare that La Beltraneja was not Enrique's daughter and therefore was ineligible to take the throne of Castile.

But before Isabella wrote to the pope, she discovered she was pregnant. The suspense was great. If the baby was a boy, La Beltraneja's claim to the throne would disappear. On June 30, 1478, Isabella gave birth to a son, named Juan for his royal grandfathers Juan of Castile and Juan of Aragón. Throughout Castile, crowds paraded and cheered. Prince Juan was baptized in the Church of Santa Maria. In a dazzling ceremony, trumpets and drums sounded as the baby boy was carried to the high altar of the church. Many interpreted this birth of a son as a sign of God's approval of the royal couple. With the keen eye of a mother, Isabella noticed that Juan was not as sturdy as his sister Isabel had been. She worried about his health and safety and hardly ever let him leave her side.

Juan's birth concluded the long war with Portugal. In 1479, after one last unsuccessful attack on Extremadura, Afonso gave up. Ambassadors for Castile and Portugal signed a peace treaty. Each leader renounced any claims to the other's crown. Under the terms of the treaty, ten-year-old Princess Isabel was to be held by a mediator for a year as a sign of her parents' good faith. Eighteen-year-old La Beltraneja was offered a choice: she could choose to wait fourteen years to marry the infant Prince Juan or she could become a nun. She chose the convent. Though they were fairly certain she would not want to wait to marry their son, which they certainly did not want to happen, Isabella and Ferdinand took the risk of making the offer in order to make themselves seem generous and forgiving. Isabella, shrewd as always, knew how to protect her own reputation.

5

The Spanish Inquisition

The royal couple was always conscious of public opinion. Instead of punishing captured rebels who had fought on Portugal's side, Isabella and Ferdinand pardoned them. It was a surprising move. But they knew that the ill treatment of conquered people usually led to more bitterness and fighting. Though some of the nobility called her weak, Isabella gambled that the freed rebels would support her when she needed it.

The next year, Isabella gave birth to her third child, Princess Juana. All told, she and Ferdinand had five children, including two more girls, Maria and Catalina. Large families were important because many children did not survive to adulthood. Isabella and Ferdinand's only disappointment was that they had only one son. Daughters were expensive because they had to be provided with large dowries when they married, although they could be valuable when arranging politically advantageous marriages.

Once the war with Portugal was over, Isabella and Ferdinand concentrated on refilling the depleted treasury. Isabella asked her confessor, the rigorous Talavera, to help retrieve properties that had once belonged to the crown. Enrique had doled them out to the *grandees* and now Isabella wanted them back. Talavera proved to be an excellent aid in this effort. His status as a holy man enabled him to appear apolitical. Soon the treasury of Castile was brimming with gold.

Isabella shared some of these new funds with the orphans and widows of soldiers killed in the Portuguese war. She also forbade the *grandees* from wearing insignias of royalty, displaying their titles publicly, or building new castles. She was intent on making sure no *grandee* tried to depose her. As always, Isabella was concerned with creating a more disciplined and orderly society. By using the power of the church and the government to strip the *grandees* of some of their power, she ensured little resistance from her subjects.

Ferdinand and Isabella worked hard but still found time to meet regularly with their court, although they did not indulge in the carousing that had been enjoyed by previous rulers. Isabella established safeguards against the misuse of judicial power by setting up a system of appeals. She also established court procedures to help to insure impartial trials. With these reforms, Isabella and Ferdinand created a powerful monarchy and the most efficient government of the time.

Opposite: This tapestry shows Ferdinand and Isabella presiding over their court.

Isabella was a confident woman. However, she was insecure about one aspect of her life—her education. Growing up as Enrique's ward, it had not seemed likely that she would ever become queen. She had been educated the way most young women were—she was well schooled in sewing and embroidery, but knew little about geography or languages or math. These inadequacies haunted her, and she made it a point to encourage learning. Not only were the members of her court forbidden to get drunk or to wear inappropriate clothing but they were also expected to be educated in music, literature, and poetry. She started a school for Juan and the other young boys in the castle and joined with her daughters to study literature, art, rhetoric, and music.

This concern with education was in some ways emblematic of the era. Although the kingdoms on the Iberian Peninsula were not powerful enough to play a large role in European diplomacy, they did occupy a crucial area. When the Moors had crossed over from Northern Africa they brought with them the classical culture of the Ancient World that had been largely neglected in most of Europe. The reasons why the scientific and artistic achievements of the Greeks, Egyptians, Romans and others had been lost to Europe are complex. The loss has been attributed to several causes: the triumph of Christianity, which tended to reject ideas outside of the Christian tradition; the chaos caused by successive waves of invaders from the east that brought about the fall of Rome; and the sheer difficulty of staying alive in the wilderness that was Europe—people fighting for their lives had little time for poetry and mathematics.

Though the Moors and the Christians did not always get along, Spanish art and architecture were strongly influenced by Moorish culture. The Renaissance came late to Spain, but other parts of Europe, such as Italy and the Netherlands, were undergoing scientific and cultural revolutions, the ripple effects of which were felt everywhere. An atmosphere of intellectual inquiry permeated the continent and Isabella was determined her country would not be left behind.

Isabella even struggled to learn Latin, at least enough so that she could correct a choir member or altar boy when necessary. Within a few years, the spirit of intellectual inquiry she fostered affected the nobility. An arts and cultural movement began in Spain. A collection of Spanish lyric poetry was published and paintings from the Flemish artists and hand-copied and printed books, including classics by Cicero and Aristotle, were placed in the royal library. Spanish courtiers were expected to be versed in Latin and the classics. Soon people from even the most cultivated areas of Europe admired the architects, writers, musicians, poets, and artists of Castile and Aragón.

Isabella loved music and often called for it in church services, military processions, and court life. The chapel that traveled with her everywhere she went included twenty singers, two organists, and a choir of about twenty-five boys. Her kingdom became known across Europe for its composers and musicians.

The royal couple welcomed the use of the new craft of printing, which had recently been invented in Germany, to their kingdom. They hoped that it would help unite Catholics by

During the Renaissance in Spain, music and art began to permeate Castilian culture. *(The National Gallery, London)*

Johannes Gutenberg is credited with developing the first printing press. This portrait depicts him standing in front of his press, holding one of the Bibles that he printed.

making it easier for church documents to be circulated. Isabella bought over four hundred newly printed volumes for herself, written in both Castilian and Latin.

The Spanish Renaissance developed mostly from inside the church. In Italy, the rebirth of interest in classical culture eventually led to more secularization as many scientists, artists, and writers became increasingly concerned with understanding the world around them than meditating on the afterlife. In Spain, however, the church's power actually increased during the Renaissance. One of the principal reasons was the influence of Isabella and Ferdinand. Another was the large population of Moors in Granada, which, along with the large Jewish population, many Catholics considered to be an intolerable situation.

One of the woeful consequences that resulted from the

Incipit epla sci Jeronimi ad pauli
nū prebiteru. de omnibus diuine hif
torie libris. Capitulum primū:

Rater ambrosius
tua michi munuscu
la perferens. detulit
sim̄l ⁊ suauissimas
litteras: que a prin
cipio amicicias fide
probate iam fidei et veteris amicicie
pferebant. Vera enī illa necessitudo ē.
et xp̄i glutino copulata: quā nō vtili
tas rei familiaris. non pñtia tantū
corporz̄ nō subdola ⁊ palpās adulatō.
sed dei timoz̄ et diuinarū scripturarū
studia conciliant. Legimus in veterib3
hiftorijs. quosdā lustrasse puincias.
nouos adijsse pplos. maria trāsisse.
ut eos quos ex libris nouerāt: corā
q̄q̄ viderent. Sic pitagoras memphi
ticos vates. sic plato egiptum ⁊ archi
tam tarentinū. eamq̄; orā ytalie. que
quondā magna grecia dicebat̄: labo
riosissime peragrauit: et ut qui athenis
mgr̄ erat. ⁊ potens. cuiusq̄; doctrinas
achademie gignasia psonabāt. fieret
peregrinus atq̄; discipulus: mal̄es a
liena verecunde discere: q̄m sua impu
denter ingerere. Deniq̄; cum litteras
quasi toto orbe fugientes persequitur
captus a piratis et venundatus. tyran
no crudelissimo paruit. ductus capti
uus vinc9 et seruus: tamen quia phi
losophus: maior emente se fuit. ad ty
tumliuiū. lacteo eloquentie fonte ma
nantem. de vltimis hispanie galliarū
q̄z finibus quosdam venisse nobiles
legimus: et quos ad cōtemplatōnem
sui roma non traxerat: vnius homi
nis fama perduxit. Habuit illa etas
inauditum omnibus seculis. celebrā
dumq̄z miraculum: ut urbem tātam

ingressi: aliud extra vrbem quererent.
Apollonius siue ille mag9 ut vulgus
loquitur. siue phus ut pitagorici tra
dunt. irrauit plas. ptrāsiuit caucasū
albānos. scithas. massagetas. opu
lentissima indie regna penetrauit: et
ad extremum latissimo physon amne
trāsmisso puenit ad bragmanas: ut
hyarcam in throno sedentē aureo. ⁊ de
tantali fonte potantem. inter paucos
disciplos. de natura. de morib3 ac de
cursu dierū ⁊ siderū audiret docentem.
Inde p elamitas. babilonios. chalde
os. medos. assirios. parthos. syros.
phenices. arabes. palestinos. reuer
sus ad alexandriā. perrexit ad ethio
piam:ut gignosophistas ⁊ famosissi
mam solis mensam videret ī sabulo.
Inuenit ille vir vbiq̄; quod disceret:⁊
semp proficiens. semper se melior fie
ret. Scripsit super hoc plenissime octo
voluminibus: phylostratus. II

Quid loquar de seculi hominib3:
cum apostolus paulus vas e
lectionis. et magister gentium. qui de
consciencia tanti in se hospitis loque
batur. dicens. An experimentum que
ritis eius qui in me loquitur cristus.
post damascum arabiāq̄; lustratam
ascenderit iherosolimā ut videret petrū
et māserit apud eum diebus quindeci.
Hoc enim misterio ebdōmadis et o
gdoadis: futur9 gentium predicator
instruendus erat. Rursumq̄; post an
nos quatuordecim assumpto barna
ba et tyto. exposuit cum apostolis eu
angelium: ne forte ī vacuum curreret
aut cucurrisset. Habet nescio quid la
tentis energie viue vocis actus: et in
aures discipuli de autoris ore trans
fusa:fort9 sonat. Vnde et eschines cū
rodi exularet. et legeret illa demostenis

strengthening of the government in Castile and Aragón was that it put more pressure on the Jewish population. In the early 1470s, Isabella and Ferdinand had revoked some of the discriminatory laws against Jews and had elevated some Jewish people to positions at court. They had ordered reluctant Christians to do business with Jews, and they had not demanded any special taxes or regulations from Jews, unlike most other European kingdoms.

This policy of relative toleration soon conflicted with the demands of the one institution that demanded and received Isabella and Ferdinand's total obedience. The Catholic Church was growing less tolerant of religious diversity. Anti-Semitism was rampant and Isabella began to believe religious unity would lead to political unity. She ordered that Christians and *conversos* restrict their contact with Jews. She also reinstated prohibitions barring Jewish land ownership, and Jews were prohibited from most occupations except money-lending.

The center of Isabella's power was Seville, a city that also happened to have a large Jewish population. Located in the fertile Andalusia region on the Guadalquivir River, Seville was an important trading center. Andalusia was renowned for its pleasant climate and the quality of the horses, cattle, and food it produced. But Seville suffered from a weak government. Isabella had traveled there in 1477, soon after being crowned queen. The citizens had welcomed her with

Opposite: The first page of the "forty-two-line Bible," the world's first printed book. This Bible is referred to as such because each page contains forty-two lines of type. The illuminations around the border were done by hand.

open arms, hoping she would restore order. At the time, law enforcement was impossible because Seville was in a state of anarchy. The city lacked proper sanitation and was rife with bribery, intimidation, uncollected taxes, and crime.

After entering the city gates, Isabella was invited to dismount her horse and was carried to the cathedral beneath a canopy of scarlet brocade, where audiences lined the streets to admire her. After several days of festivities including jousts, bullfights, and dances, she established a court with herself as chief magistrate. She set up a strong police force and ordered it to be vigilant in rooting out crime and handing down severe sentences. Sevillians began to fear her. A group of nobles sent the bishop to talk her out of the harsh punishments she was meting out. Isabella agreed to issue a general pardon to any criminal who made restitution to his victims, but vowed that heretics would not be forgiven under any circumstances.

Isabella was alarmed by a Dominican priest's report that some *conversos* were secretly practicing Judaism in Seville. Local members of the clergy and church officials in Rome prodded her to investigate. In 1478, Pope Sixtus IV granted her permission to appoint several priests to look into the allegations of blasphemy against the church. These investigations were the beginning of the Spanish Inquisition. Directed by the Catholic Monarchs, the name often given to Isabella and Ferdinand, it would systematically arrest and put on trial all non-converted Jews or suspicious *conversos*. Anyone who refused to convert, or who was deemed to be a Christian in name only, was to be executed.

Pope Sixtus IV, above, authorized Isabella to implement the Inquisition.

While a heretic was anyone who questioned the church and its doctrines, the Inquisition focused most of its terrible force on the *conversos*, because many suspected that some *conversos* were secretly practicing Judaism.

The unconverted Jews were also persecuted, both within and without the official capacity of the Inquisition, but they could not technically be tried as heretics because they had never been baptized into the Catholic faith. Rather, they were denounced and threatened because of their religion. The church considered Judaism to be an abomination be-cause according to church doctrine, the Jews had been given the opportunity to accept Jesus of Nazareth as the chosen one, the promised Messiah, but had rejected that chance. Because of that rejection, the new chosen people were the Christians, and they saw Judaism as a heresy. The heretic had two choices—convert wholeheartedly, or die.

Though Isabella had the power to open an Inquisition in Seville, she did not do so. One reason for the delay was that Afonso and La Beltraneja were still contesting her claim to the throne. There was too much unrest among the citizens to risk losing control of a state-run campaign of terror. But popular hatred of the Jews could not be denied indefinitely. Reports of heresy and complaints about Jews piled up until Isabella could ignore them no longer. To do so, she worried, would be to commit heresy herself.

The queen had some sympathy for the *conversos*. She believed the reason most did not embrace Christianity was because of a failure of childhood training. She ordered two cardinals to instruct potential *conversos* on religion. These cardinals and other church officials focused on the idea that Jews could avoid perpetual damnation if they converted. Many *conversos* did become faithful Christians. Others would not totally renounce their heritage.

By 1480, Isabella and Ferdinand conceded that they had not been able to adequately reach the *conversos*. Isabella had promised her confessor that she would devote herself "to the extirpation of heresy, for the glory of God and the exaltation of the Catholic faith." This promise weighed heavily on her mind. Seeing no other options, she implemented the papal bull authorizing her to begin an Inquisition.

The Spanish Inquisition had leaders but it needed the cooperation of Spanish subjects to be truly effective. Both common citizens and church leaders set up anonymous spy systems. All Christians were expected to identify possible heretics. They were given a list of thirty-seven ways to spot one, which included activities as unremarkable as avoiding pork or wearing particularly nice clothes on Saturday (the Jewish holy day). Any Christian who suspected heresy and did not report it could be condemned to death and to eternal damnation. The threat of the Inquisition so terrified citizens that nearly five thousand fled Seville as soon as it was announced. Others confessed to heresy, and still others would maintain their innocence even after being accused.

The accused were considered guilty until proven innocent—and they were not allowed to know who had accused them. This system made accusations a convenient way to eliminate one's enemies. Torture was an accepted means of exacting confessions. Even if accused heretics confessed and said they repented, they were often subjected to further imprisonment, whipping, and other forms of torture. So many were burned at the stake that a field outside Seville was designated as the *quemadero,* or burning field. No one is sure how many died from the Inquisition in Seville, but estimates range up to nine thousand between the years 1480 and 1488. The inquisitors believed that it was important for all people in the area to witness the punishment of heretics. Sometimes they arranged a long procession that wound slowly through the streets of the town. At the head of the procession were the inquisitors themselves. Then came the

heretics being led to their punishment. Clerics in the procession carried simulations of burned heretics and their bones.

The Inquisition was devastating to the people and the economy of Castile. Many of those who fled or were killed had been influential in business, and losing them damaged the economy. Cloth and silk markets disappeared, shops were abandoned, and trade diminished. Isabella accepted this news calmly in the belief that the cleansing of the country of heretics was more important than any economic disruptions. Consequently, Spain becam a country forged by bloodshed and misery.

Opposite: This famous painting by Pedro Berruguete depicts an Inquisition trial, called an *auto-da-fe,* or an "act of faith." *(The Prado Museum, Madrid)*

6

War against the Moors

The Spanish Inquisition was intrinsically connected to the centuries of conflict the Christians had with the Moors. Seven hundred years before Isabella's reign, Muslims from North Africa had invaded the Iberian Peninsula. The Visigoths, one of the groups that had invaded Europe from the east in the last years of the Roman Empire, controlled most of the area when the Muslims began pouring across the Strait of Gibraltar in the seventh century. In 711, the Muslim forces defeated the Goths and over the next few years the remnant of the defeated Visigoth army retreated to the mountains. This left the majority of the Christian population to live under the control of the Muslims, who were called Moors.

Over time the Moor rulers were weakened by internal dissension. This coincided with a revitalization of Christian

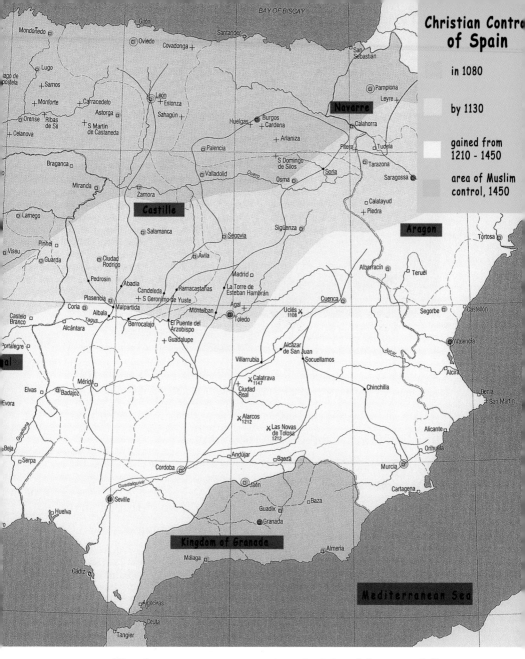

Christian Contro
of Spain

in 1080

by 1130

gained from
1210 - 1450

area of Muslim
control, 1450

BAY OF BISCAY

Mondoñedo

Gijón

Santander

Oviedo
Covadonga

San
Sebastian

iago de
postela

Lugo

Samos

León
Eslonza

Pamplona

Leyre

Monforte
Carracedelo

Astorga

Sahagún

Navarre

Calahorra

Orense
Ribas
de Sil

S Martin
de Castaneda

Huelgas
Burgos
Cardena

Celanova

Palencia

Arlanza

Pitero

Tudela

Braganca

S Domingo
de Silos

Tarazona

Miranda

Valladolid

Duero

Osma

Soria

Saragossa

Zamora

Calatayud

Piedra

Lamego

Castille

Salamanca

Segovia

Sigüenza

Aragon

Tortosa

Pinhel

Viseu

Guarda

Ciudad
Rodrigo

Avila

Albarracín

Teruèl

Pedrosin

Abadia
Candeleda

Ramacastañas

La Torre de
Esteban Hambrán

Madrid

Cuenca

Segorbe

Castellón

Plasencia
S Geronimo de Yuste

Malpartida

Montalban

Agal

Uclés
1108

Coria
Albala

Tagus

Berrocalajo

El Puente del
Arzobispo

Toledo

Castelo
Branco

Alcántara

Guadalupe

Alcázar
de San Juan

Jucar

Valencia

Portalegre

Villarrubia

Socuellamos

Alcira

Elvas

Mérida

Badajoz

Calatrava
1147
Ciudad
Real

Chinchilla

Denia
San Martin

Evora

Alarcos
1212

Las Novas
de Tolosa
1212

Alicante

Beja

Andújar

Baeza

Murcia

Orihuela

Serpa

Cordoba

Guadalquivir

Jaén

Baza

Cartagena

Seville

Guadix

Granada

Huelva

Kingdom of Granada

Almeria

Málaga

Cádiz

Mediterranean Sea

Agéciras

Ceuta

Tangier

power. Slowly, over seven centuries, the Moorish states fell
to Christians. By the time the great king Ferdinand III, the
Saint, died in 1252, the Moors had been contained in the
kingdom of Granada, on the southeastern tip of the Iberian
Peninsula, where they remained when Ferdinand and Isabella

A view of the Moorish masterpiece in Granada, the Alhambra.

assumed control of Castile. Granada was important as a center of commerce and as a pathway for merchants traveling both east and west. There the Moors had built forts, mosques, schools, and a fortress famed throughout Europe, the magnificent and ornate Alhambra.

There had been a long period of tense coexistence between Granada and the rest of Spain. Then, beginning in 1476, the king of Granada, Ali Abu al-Hasan, refused to pay the tribute demanded by Isabella and Ferdinand. Abu al-Hasan gambled that the new monarchs were too busy fighting the war of succession with the Portuguese and then reforming their joint kingdoms to risk war with Granada. He also took advantage of their troubles by mounting raids on border cities, leading to several skirmishes between Muslim and Christian soldiers. Finally, in December of 1481, Hasan's troops scaled the walls of the Castilian city of Zahara. Zahara had long been considered to be impregnable, but the Moorish soldiers proved otherwise. Once inside the walled mountaintop city, they claimed it for the

A view of the Moorish stronghold of Granada from the town of Alhama. *(Courtesy of Art Resource.)*

Moorish kingdom and sent about one hundred and fifty men, women, and children back to Granada as slaves.

Ferdinand and Isabella decided that they could not tolerate Hasan's aggression any longer. To do so made them look weak, which would invite further attacks. They also considered a campaign against the Moors to be a natural extension of the Holy War against the Jews. Only days after receiving the news from Zahara, they declared their intention of driving the last of the Moors from Spain.

The first official battle of the Christian reconquest was an attack on Alhama, a city in Granada. In just one day, Castilian battering rams broke down the gates of Alhama. Soldiers entered behind a shower of poisoned arrows, lead balls, and boiling oil. Thousands of Muslims were killed or wounded. The Castilian general ordered his troops to throw the dead bodies over the city walls. The next morning, Abu al-Hasan arrived with eight thousand men. They were so enraged by the sight of the dead Moors being eaten by vultures and wild dogs that, foolishly, the soldiers scrambled to the top of Alhama's walls where Castilian spears and arrows quickly cut them down.

Once the Moors overcame their initial emotional reaction, they settled down to a more shrewd strategy. The only water supply lay outside of the city's walls. The Moors planned to force the Christians out by cutting off their access to water. Their plan proved very effective, and by the time Ferdinand was able to summon an army and rush to assist the Castilian troops, they were in dire straits. Ferdinand suggested abandoning the city but Isabella refused to back down. Alhama, she said, was "the first place we have conquered" and therefore they would "keep it by all means."

Travelling slowly because she was in the second trimester of another pregnancy, Isabella followed her husband to the battlefield. She established a base nearby and served as his quartermaster. Keeping track of troops and supplies, she used her administrative and organizational skills to ensure that Ferdinand's army had everything it needed. Less than six months after the initial attack, the Moorish troops withdrew and Castilian armies established their authority in the city. Isabella had already ordered the supplies necessary to convert the Muslim mosques into churches. The Catholic Monarchs had won the first victory in this Holy War.

Buoyed by this initial victory, Ferdinand and his troops marched deeper into Moorish territory. Although Isabella was far along in her pregnancy, she followed. To supply and feed the army she gathered cartloads of wheat, chickens, sheep, and wine. She enlisted the support of *grandees* who agreed to provide their own men and equipment on the condition that they would be awarded some of the conquered territory. In the midst of the excitement, Isabella's fourth pregnancy came to term. She delivered a blond daughter, Maria, then, thirty-five hours later, delivered a stillborn girl, Maria's twin.

Over the next few years, the Castilian troops suffered several terrible defeats. Ferdinand was forced to rethink his military tactics and adapt them to the difficult terrain. His enemy had a superior knowledge of the land. He needed heavy artillery, lots of supplies, and well-trained soldiers to succeed. Isabella saw that he got what he needed, and Ferdinand moved into Granada with greater zeal.

Ferdinand attacked through the towns of Baeza, Jaén, Cujar, and Córdoba. The Moors fought bravely at every turn. The hot summer weather was relentless. Ferdinand conducted a labor-intensive but conservative campaign. Instead of attacking cities directly, his men would first arduously clear the surrounding fields. They felled trees and pulled up brush in order to create deep trenches. After cutting them off from reinforcements and supplies, they laid siege to the isolated cities. The goal was to starve the citizens into submission. Their methods were time-consuming and crude, but effective.

Isabella was an indispensable military partner, serving as provisioner, quartermaster, behind-the-scenes administrator, and morale booster. She obtained scores of heavy guns and cannons, and loaded countless mule trains with flour, dried fish, and cured meat to feed her soldiers. She ordered war drums to inspire the Castilians and bells to frighten the Moors, who were superstitious about the sound of bells. She acquired doctors, beds, clothes, and medicines, and established a queen's hospital to travel with the fighting men. This was the first military hospital in western Europe. When she visited wounded and dying soldiers, she told them to be thankful that they had been given the opportunity to cleanse their land of heresy.

Autumn brought hurricanes that made it difficult to rebuild bridges and roads. The Castilian suppliers found it more and more difficult to hack out mule paths from the muddy earth. More men were needed, and more men meant more supplies.

Ferdinand and Isabella's newly refilled treasury ran low. Soon, there were no more *grandees* to volunteer money. She had to pawn her jewels, including the ones that Ferdinand had given her at their wedding. The jewels bought food, warm clothes, and munitions, but the new supplies did not raise the spirits of the soldiers. They were weary of war and discouraged by rampant illness. It took Isabella to renew their faith. Once she recovered from Maria's birth, Isabella began visiting the troops. Her reputation was such that she could inspire them to fight as they never had before. Many people believed that Isabella was the incarnation of the

Virgin Mary, and that she had been divinely appointed to the throne. The Moors were terrified of her. As her procession approached the Castilian encampment outside one Moorish city, the people of the city became so frightened they surrendered three days later.

A turning point in the war came in March 1483, when Castilian soldiers captured Abu al-Hasan's son, usually known as Boabdil, who was at war with his father over who should rule Granada. Boabdil, who had only recently escaped from the tower in which his father had imprisoned him, was more like Isabella's half-brother Enrique than his own father—or Ferdinand. He preferred the company of his favorite courtesans to fighting and was unpopular in his own country. Still, his capture was a great boon for the Castilians.

The royal council held several intense discussions about

Boabdil, the last king of Granada.

Boabdil's fate. Some advocated punishing him as an example, others argued he should be freed in hopes that he would continue to fight his father. When no agreement could be reached, the decision had to be left to Isabella, the queen. She ordered that he be given the chance to agree to a treaty.

Isabella promised Boabdil that he would be released if he agreed to certain conditions. He had to promise to support Ferdinand and to persuade other Moors to do the same. He had to sign a two-year treaty of peace and pay an annual tribute to Castile. He had to allow Castilian soldiers to pass through his land and to supply them with provisions. In order to ensure Boabdil's cooperation, his sons would be kept as hostages at Isabella and Ferdinand's court.

Boabdil agreed, believing the treaty would help him in his fight against his father. Ferdinand and Isabella gave him gifts and treated him like an equal to celebrate their new partnership, then returned him in royal fashion to Granada. Though Boabdil did not have the popular support his father did, he did uphold his end of the bargain and, in doing so, helped Castile gain an advantage in the war.

The war finally seemed to be turning in their favor. Isabella was pleased at the progress her troops were making. She had promised the church that she would eliminate the infidels from the peninsula and it looked like she would soon be able to deliver on that promise. She was therefore extremely angry when Ferdinand proposed putting the war against the Moors on hold in order to fight another one.

Ferdinand's father, King Juan of Aragón, had died in 1479. Ferdinand had inherited his title. In accordance with his marriage contract, Ferdinand had left behind his own lands in order to serve Castile. Now he wanted to return to his home. Aragón's northern border was the Pyrenees Mountains. On the other side of the mountains was France, which had long claimed two Aragónese provinces that lay in the shadow of the Pyrenees, Roussillon and Cerdagne. Ferdinand and his father had been determined to win them back. In 1483, the news came that the king of France had died—and that on his deathbed, he had given instructions to return Roussillon and Cerdagne to Aragón. When it became apparent the king's heirs were unwilling to fulfill his promise, Ferdinand wanted to seize the provinces. Now was the time, he insisted, before the new French rulers consolidated power. He had been fighting for Castile since his marriage, he said, and now he wanted to win a victory for his own country. Isabella argued with her husband vehemently. Though she was sympathetic to Ferdinand's feelings, seizing land from another Catholic kingdom could wait. There was nothing more important than Holy War against the infidels.

Map of the contested territories of Aragón on the French border.

It is a sign of the respect the couple had for each other that they were able to settle this disagreement peacefully. Though Isabella, as the more powerful ruler, could have instructed Ferdinand to abandon the Aragónese cause, she did not. Instead, she offered to lend him some troops but made it clear she would be returning to the war in Granada in the meantime—with or without him. Ferdinand would have to solicit funds for a war with the French from the *cortes*. Isabella would not interfere with their decision. In the end, it was the *cortes* that denied Ferdinand the support he needed to win back Roussillon and Cerdagne. The frustrated king had little choice but to return to battle against the Moors. The Aragónese cause would have to wait.

The reunited royal couple attacked the Moors with renewed vigor. In the winter of 1484-5, Isabella and Ferdinand launched their greatest military effort. They planned a new kind of warfare, leaving behind old-fashioned lances, swords, and battering rams. The new equipment they commissioned was fashioned by blacksmiths and engineers and included especially powerful cannons called lombards. Isabella financed this new initiative by again soliciting funds from the Catholic Church. Because she was engaged in a Holy War, she argued, the church should help her cause. Castilian troops were reinforced by members of the Swiss Guard, an elite mercenary force that fought only for Christian causes on the orders of the pope. The Swiss Guard was legendary; its presence alone helped to cow the enemy.

Ferdinand set his sights on the city of Ronda, on the

southern tip of Granada. Controlling Ronda would give his armies easier access to the rest of the Moorish lands and help block shipments of aid from Northern Africa. Isabella set up relay stations to transport massive amounts of supplies to the soldiers. Ronda surrendered after a two-week siege. Isabella expelled all the resi-

The Tajo gorge in the dramatic cliff town of Ronda.

dents, allowing them to take only what they could carry. She apportioned the exiles' property and buildings to Castilians who wanted to settle there. The mosques became churches and cathedrals equipped grandly with bells, chalices, crosses, and brocade vestments. Masses of thanksgiving were observed in cities throughout Spain.

Castilian troops were able to free nearly two hundred prisoners from Ronda, some of whom had been held for two years. Queen Isabella was there to greet each one. After the ceremony she asked the ex-prisoners to hang the rusty iron handcuffs they had worn on the walls of the largest church in Toledo. The old manacles are still there today.

This map of southern Europe and the Middle East shows the holdings of the Ottoman Empire at the end of the fifteenth century.

Internal divisions weakened Granada further. Boabdil and his father, King Hasan, now faced competition for leadership from Hasan's brother, known as El Zagal. When Hasan's age and infirmity prevented him from leading his troops, El Zagal, rather than Boabdil, was the popular choice for a new leader. He took up the Moorish cause with such vehemence that the Castilians were dealt several painful defeats.

El Zagal's success inspired Muslim leaders from the east to lend their support. The Ottoman Turks, who ruled most of the Muslim lands in the Middle East and Eastern Europe, sent ships from their powerful armada to the shores of Ferdinand's island kingdom of Sicily. Pope Innocent VIII, who had been installed at the death of Pope Sixtus IV, granted Ferdinand and Isabella a new Bull of Crusade that allowed them to take church monies from Castilian tithes to fund a renewed attack on the Moors.

In 1485, Boabdil broke his promise of loyalty to Ferdinand

and Isabella and seized the town of Loja. Ferdinand took it back from him in 1486. Boabdil was captured again, and yet again released. Though neither Ferdinand nor Isabella trusted him, they believed he could distract the Moors. Abu al-Hasan had died and Boabdil was now king—if El Zagal wanted that title he would have to fight both the Castilians and his own nephew.

Isabella celebrated the victory at Loja by walking to the church barefoot to offer prayers of thanksgiving. Then, despite the danger, she visited the military camp near the city walls where she was greeted by the soldiers as an instrument of God who would free the land from the infidel. The Castilian army stood at attention as she passed by wearing rich crimson brocade and velvet. She told the

A battle between the Moors and the Christians during the reconquest in southern Spain.

assembled knights, "God knows our cause and will not forget our difficulties and will remember them in the other [world]." She spent time in hospitals visiting the sick and offering prayers for their recovery.

After the victory at Loja, Isabella sent orders to amass supplies of iron, cattle, and munitions for the next attack. Although Isabella grieved at the loss of life that the war was causing, she believed the war was God's will. There is no exact tally of how many people were killed during the ten-year conflict, but the fighting took an enormous toll on the people and the land.

By April of 1491, Ferdinand had amassed 50,000 men, including reinforcements from England, Germany, Switzerland, France, and Burgundy—all kingdoms eager to participate in a victory over the Muslims. His troops had made enough inroads to finally lay siege to the city of Granada itself—which was now held by Boabdil.

As usual, Ferdinand's plan was to minimize the fighting and use patience to draw his enemy out. Castilian soldiers surrounded the city and prevented any supplies from entering. He and Isabella agreed "Hunger alone will win the city for us."

Forty-year-old Isabella was following the war closely. Though she could not lead the troops into battle because she was a woman, she arrived at the military camp dressed in full armor and mounted a warhorse to review them. The soldiers greeted her with cheers and music. Always aware of the effect her presence had on the men, Isabella, dressed in her finery, visited wounded soldiers in the hospital she

This painting by Francisco Pradilla shows Boabdil handing over the keys of the city to Ferdinand and Isabella at the surrender of Granada in 1492. *(Courtesy of Art Resource.)*

had created. She spoke to the troops and urged them to continue the fight for Spain and for Christianity.

In early January 1492, Boabdil sent messengers to the Castilian camp. He was ready to surrender. His own people had turned against him, his forces were greatly outnumbered, and his populace was starving. Ferdinand met Boabdil on the road outside Granada to accept the keys to the city. Boabdil agreed to leave Granada and to make a new home in exile. Before he crested the hill on the road away from the last Muslim holdout on the Iberian Peninsula, Boabdil turned for a final look at the city. Today that hill is still called *El Ultimo Sospiro del Moro,* The Last Sigh of the Moor.

On January 6, Ferdinand and Isabella entered Granada

Isabella and Ferdinand riding up to the newly consecrated cathedral of Granada after the surrender of Boabdil.

for the first time. Their grand procession was full of all the finery and flags they could muster. They moved solemnly through the city streets, pausing to admire the fourteenth century palace, the Alhambra, a wonder of stone lacework, richly decorated walls, and intricate carvings. They attended a High Mass of thanksgiving at a newly consecrated former mosque. Isabella sent out the message that the victory was a mighty achievement: "We assure you that this city of Granada is greater in population than you can imagine; the royal palace very grand and the richest in Spain."

7

The Expulsion of the Jews

The reconquest of Spain from the Moors, the *reconquista,* almost eight hundred years in the making, had finally been accomplished. Isabella and Ferdinand wanted to capitalize on their advantage over the Moors and send troops into North Africa and push the Muslims even farther east. But, in the end, they decided that the venture would dangerously overextend their resources. Their people were weary of fighting and dying. Instead, they decided to spend much less money on a much riskier expedition—they would send an ambitious young Italian sailor off to find a shorter trade route to the east.

Internationally, the conquest of Granada was regarded as a great advance for Christianity. It was a fitting retaliation for the 1453 Muslim conquest of Constantinople, the last Christian city left in the old Byzantine Empire. The victory was a financial boon as well—Granada's large Moorish population and healthy economy would boost Castile's empty treasury. In an effort to quell a growing trend toward enslaving Muslims, Isabella and Ferdinand instructed all who were holding Muslim captives as slaves to turn them over to royal officials. The crown would reimburse them for their loss.

Though Isabella had fought the war to eliminate a non-Christian religion from the region, she realized that forcing Catholicism onto the remaining Moorish population would only alienate them further from their new rulers. So the treaty Isabella approved stipulated that the Moors would be allowed to practice their religion and that their lifestyles would generally continue as they had before. They would not be required to pay any more in taxes than they had under Boabdil, and they would maintain their current system of government.

However, Isabella and her advisors implemented a system designed to bring as many Muslims as possible into the Catholic faith. They barred the Inquisition from Granada for forty years to encourage true conversions. They took as their motto, "What is done for fear and by force cannot long endure, while what is done for love and charity is enduring." Isabella ordered the establishment of an Arabic school for Christian clergy and had some of the Catholic canon translated into Arabic.

It is possible the Moors and the conquering Christians could have established a lasting peace, if not for the inherent conflict of their religions. The Inquisition that had begun in

Seville was spreading across the kingdom. With it came corruption, death, and torture. Anyone could accuse anyone else of being a heretic—and since the Inquisition was conducted in such a way that victims could not confront their accusers, few were able to successfully deny the charges. If the accused confessed to the crime, and even more so if they were able to name others, they were usually allowed to live—though they were tortured and often imprisoned. If the accused maintained their innocence, the result was usually public humiliation followed by torture or burning at the stake. As the Inquisition spread from Seville, panicked citizens fled or accused others in order to protect their own lives.

A drawing of three men who were convicted by the Inquisition.

RTRAITS DE 3 HOMMES CONDAMNÉES PAR L'INQUISITION D'EPAGNE

This oil portrait, painted nearly four hundred years after the beginning of the Inquisition, shows Pope Sixtus IV meeting with one of the inquisitors, Tomás de Torquemada. The pope and the inquisitors worked closely together to coordinate the Inquisition in Seville and elsewhere. *(Courtesy of Art Resource.)*

In February 1481, three prominent residents of Seville were burned at the stake for heresy. They were *conversos* who had felt safe because of their presumed conversion and because of their wealth. They were tried in a church ceremony known as an *auto-da-fe,* or act of faith, and were burned at the stake. The people of Seville went into a panic and fear ruled the city. The Inquisition seemed to be spinning out of control—no one was safe.

The next year, four years after he sanctioned the Inquisition in Spain, Pope Sixtus IV declared that he would send his hand-chosen inquisitors to Seville to take control. He had received several reports that the interrogations there was being conducted with unusual brutality. He explained, "The Inquisition has for some time been moved not by zeal for the faith and the salvation of souls, but by lust and wealth." The pope was referring to the fact that those who were accused usually had their property seized—either by their accusers, thus providing a clear motivation for making baseless accusations—or by the state. The pope was also concerned that Spanish Inquisitors were not offering the traditional edict of grace—a period during which anyone who confessed would be asked to pay a penance but would be otherwise forgiven. Isabella denied Pope Sixtus's accusations. Ferdinand warned the pope not to interfere: "Take care . . . [to] entrust us with the care of this question." The Catholic Monarchs did not plan to give up the Spanish Catholic Church to the pope. They hoped to keep its power and money for themselves.

By 1483, the war with the Moors had created a climate of religious intolerance and fear. Nevertheless, the Jewish community was surprised at Ferdinand and Isabella's edict, which was issued on the first day of the new year, that all Jews living in Seville and Córdoba had one month to leave. Within a year, thousands of Jews had moved from Castile after selling their homes and possessions at a fraction of their value. They sought refuge in Extremadura, Portugal, and even Granada.

Now the pope insisted that church officials should be in

control of the Inquisition. He established his own investigation into the alleged abuses and appointed Tomás de Torquemada the Grand Inquisitor of Spain.

Torquemada was well known as an uncompromising priest. He wore a hair shirt, fasted regularly, and slept on a hard board, all in hopes of achieving spiritual grace. He was also well known for his hatred of Jews and *conversos.*

Despite the pope's desire for reform, there was little to distinguish Torquemada's Inquisition from the one that Isabella and Ferdinand had presided over. Torture, beating, and burning at the stake were commonplace. People continued to flee the country, either out of guilt or fear, and an atmosphere of distrust pervaded the kingdom. Despite continuing public protests, Isabella and Ferdinand supported Torquemada. They were convinced the Inquisition was the only way to save Christianity and to create a united Spain. They saw it as a natural extension of the Holy War they were fighting in the south.

Torquemada raised anti-Semitism to a new level of hatred. *Conversos* who were suspected of secretly practicing Judaism were the main targets. The public hysteria was so intense that strange and bizarre stories spread like fire. In one incident, several *conversos* and a practicing Jew were implicated in the alleged crucifixion of a young boy. What made the story so unusual was that some of the men voluntarily confessed to the crime, even though investigators could find no evidence it had even taken place—or that the boy had ever existed. No parents ever came forward to say their son was missing, and no body was found. Yet all

Torquemada's zealous approach to the Inquisition resulted in the torture, burning, and hanging of thousands of Jews in Spain. *(Courtesy of Art Resource.)*

the men involved were burned at the stake. The *conversos* re-embraced Christianity before they died, thus earning the right to be mercifully strangled before the fire was lit. The Jewish man refused conversion and was tortured and then burned alive.

Tensions were so high after these events that some Jewish leaders appealed to Isabella and Ferdinand for help. In response, the monarchs granted the Jews a letter of safe conduct to leave the country. The letter stated that the reason for the safe conduct was that Jews had recently been subjected "to much abuse and mistreatment . . . we beg that they be treated mercifully and with justice." This statement did not stop the persecution, but it may have saved some who were able to make their way out of the country.

Torquemada continued to spread tales of evil infidels and heretics. The people of Spain were infected with hatred and fear. Some prominent Jews begged Ferdinand for help: "Please, O King. What is it that you want from your subjects: Ask us anything; presents of gold and silver and whatever you want from the house of Israel that we can give to your native land." Ferdinand gave no answer. In March 1492, he and Isabella signed an Edict of Expulsion stating that all Jews who refused baptism must leave Castile and Aragón within three months.

Granada had fallen to the Castilians just a few months earlier. Ferdinand and Isabella were flushed with triumph. The Muslim war had been a Holy War, and its goal, they claimed, was to make Spain a Christian nation. Eliminating the Jews from Spain seemed to be the next logical step. The monarchs knew public opinion was against the Jews. Torquemada, too, was in favor of this extreme measure. When Isabella and Ferdinand met with Jewish leaders to discuss their plans, Torquemada burst into the meeting and threw a heavy silver cross on the table. His message was clear: Spain was a Catholic kingdom, and only Catholics were welcome.

Isabella organized the expulsion of the Jews as efficiently as she had quartermastered the army. She ordered the kingdom to pay any and all debts it owed to Jews, and she provided letters of safe conduct. However, the expelled Jews were allowed to take only as much property as they could carry and had to sell the rest. They were forbidden to take any arms, horses, gold, silver, or money. Christians quickly realized that they could buy Jewish property and businesses very cheaply. One curate wrote that it was not uncommon to see "a house [given] in exchange for an ass, and a vineyard for a length of cloth or linen."

Anywhere from 75,000 to 200,000 Jews hurried out of cities and towns to make their way to the ports or over the mountains into Europe. One writer reported that they left "by the roads and fields with so much labor and ill fortune, some collapsing, others getting up, some dying, others giving birth, others falling ill, so that there was no Christian who was not sorry for them." Families who had lived on the Iberian Peninsula for a thousand years were cast out into the world defenseless, poor, and alone.

Rumors quickly spread that Jews had resorted to desperate measures, including ingesting coins and jewels, in order to sneak some of their money out of the country. Checkpoints were set up and searches conducted. Jews were routinely robbed and killed. Corpses were found with their guts slashed open as hopeful robbers probed their stomachs for hidden treasure. Some who boarded ships made it safely to North Africa or Turkey or Greece; others were robbed by pirates or taken prisoner and sold into slavery. Ferdinand and Isabella presided over one of the most tragic and brutal pogroms in history.

8

Columbus

In the first eighteen years Ferdinand and Isabella had ruled Castile, they managed to conquer the Moors and to drive out the Jews. They had established a strong central government, created a police force to keep order, and enriched the government's coffers while keeping in check the power of the nobility and the Catholic Church. The Renaissance was bringing rapid cultural and intellectual development. Though the Inquisition continued—it was not formally ended until 1834—the kingdom was at peace for the first time in their reign.

In December of 1485, a blue-eyed Genoese navigator, Christopher Columbus (born Cristobal Colón) appeared in Castile to ask for advice and help. The thirty-five-year-old sailor told the Castilian court he had a way to reach the East by sailing west. Ever since the Ottoman Turks had taken

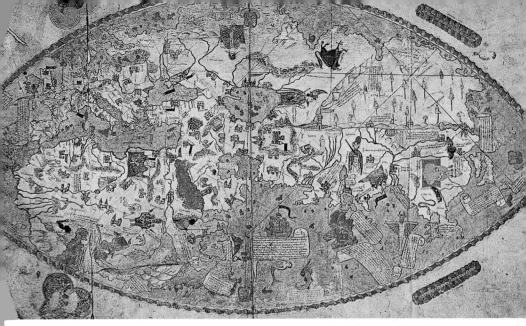

This map, called the Toscanelli Planisphere, was created in Italy around 1457. At the time, Africa had yet to be circumnavigated and the Americas had not even been imagined. It is thought that the planisphere had a profound effect on Columbus's ideas and theories. *(National Library, Florence)*

Constantinople in 1453, access to the lucrative spice trade of the Far East had been difficult and expensive to maintain. Everyone was eager to find another route to get to the Orient. Columbus was not the only one looking for a new Eastern route, but his drive and persistence set him apart from the others.

Columbus was charming and eloquent and well regarded as a seaman. Like most of his contemporaries, he thought Earth to be roughly spherical in shape. Though a few people held on to ancient beliefs that the earth was flat and that anyone who sailed too far would fall off, Columbus and other seaman had observed the curve of the horizon and concluded that Earth must be round. What they did not know was the exact size of the planet. No one knew for certain what existed over the western horizon, but Columbus was convinced he could sail west and eventually come ashore in the Indies. Others thought Earth was so large that it was impossible to make such a long sea voyage.

Columbus tried for months to meet with the Spanish rulers. He was finally granted an audience with Ferdinand and Isabella in the spring of 1486. At that meeting he asked them to fund his exploratory journey, saying simply "Our Lord revealed to me that it was feasible to sail from here to the Indies. Filled with this fire I came to your Highnesses." What he did not mention was the large number of other potential benefactors that had already turned him down.

Isabella was interested in Columbus's proposition. She asked that a committee, headed by her most trusted confessor, the priest Talavera, be set up to review the project. She wanted to know what the experts thought, but she also

CHRISTOPHER COLUMBUS

Christopher Columbus (1451-1506) was born the oldest child in his family in the Italian port city of Genoa. Christopher worked with his father in the family wool-selling business. He had an early interest in cartography and in the sea.

In 1474, Columbus signed on to a ship. For the first two years he sailed mostly in the Mediterranean and Agean seas, but in 1476 he made his first voyage on the Atlantic Ocean.

Although there were no official portraits painted of Columbus during his lifetime, many composite images have given historians a good idea of what the Genoese sailor looked like.

On this trip his ship was attacked by privateers and sunk. Columbus survived only by swimming more than six miles to shore.

After this first Atlantic adventure Columbus lived for some time in Lisbon, Portugal, one of the most active maritime centers in Europe. He was joined there by his brother Bartolomeo, who made his living as a mapmaker. Columbus became an active sailor, making voyages along the African coast and as far north as Iceland and Ireland. He married the daughter of a prominent Portuguese family in 1479, but she died in 1485. The couple had a son, Diego Colón. Later, Columbus had a child by a woman he did not marry.

Sometime around 1480, Columbus conceived of his plan to sail west across the Atlantic to reach Asia. This was an alternative route to the long, dangerous voyage south and east around Africa. The sailor first tried to interest the Portuguese king in his scheme, but experts were able to convince the king to reject the plan. He then turned to Isabella and Ferdinand, who finally agreed to fund him in 1492. Along with most of the funding, he was granted the title Admiral of the Ocean Sea and given governorship of any lands he discovered as well as participation in any profits. The first voyage left Spain on August 3. After stopping in the Canary Islands for provisions, he sailed west with his three ships—*Niña, Pinta,* and *Santa Maria.*

Christopher Columbus's coat of arms incorporated the lion and castle of Isabella's arms.

Columbus's ships were each rigged with square sails that were better suited to the dominant winds of the mid-Atlantic than was the traditional lanteen rigging that used a slanting triangular sail ideal for short passages requiring more maneuvering ablility. None of the vessels had a dead weight of more than eighty tons, and each carried a crew of approximately thirty men. While the *Niña* and the *Pinta* were only seventy feet long, Columbus's flagship, the *Santa Maria,* was a bit longer at seventy-five feet, with a deeper draft that made the ship less fit for exploration near reefs or shallow island waters. In fact, the *Santa Maria* eventually ran aground in the Caribbean and had to be abandoned.

It is not known for certain exactly where Columbus first landed. It was probably on San Salvador Island in the Bahamas on October 12, 1492. He quickly encountered, apparently within twenty-four hours, peaceful natives. On the first trip he also made it to the coast of Cuba and other islands. He remained convinced he had discovered a faster route to Asia. Before returning to Spain, he founded a settlement and left men behind.

The second voyage lasted from 1493 until 1496. This time the Admiral of the Ocean Sea left with seventeen ships and over a thousand men. The goal was to seize the land and to covert the natives to loyal Christain subjects of Spain. When he arrived at the outpost he had left behind he discovered that the men there had been killed in a fight with the natives. He established another settlement and spent a great deal of time exploring Cuba and Jamacia. He also altered his earlier more peaceful attitude toward the natives, who he now saw as being much more aggressive than he had earlier thought. He took several hundred into slavery and shipped them back to Spain. Many died on the journey across the Atlantic. Many of the natives in present-day Haiti were ordered to find gold. When he began to worry that gold was not as plentiful as originally thought, Columbus began to advocate the importation of slaves to Europe, but the Spanish monarchs rejected the plans. Nevertheless, a system was established that made the natives virtual slaves to the Spanish. Many were worked to death and thousands more died of diseases introduced by the Europeans for which they had not developed immunities.

Columbus returned to Spain in 1496, where he remained for almost two years. He made his third voyage to the New World in 1498. On this trip he discovered the mainland of South America. Although he seemed to have developed doubts, he remained convinced to his death that he had landed on a previously unknown part of Asia.

On this trip Columbus discovered that many of the original settlers were upset that the vast riches they had been promised had not materialized. Not only did Columbus have to deal with an increasingly dissatisfied native population, but there were rebellions and anger among the Europeans. He had some dissenters hanged; others returned to Spain and reported to the king and queen that Columbus was corrupt. An emissary, Francisco de Bobadilla, was sent from Spain in 1500. He quickly arrested Columbus, along with his brother who had accompanied him on his voyages, and returned them as prisoners to Spain. Columbus was later freed, but was stripped of his official titles.

Columbus, along with his son, made a final voyage from 1502 to 1504. He landed in Central America, where he encountered natives of Mesoamerica. He was soon stranded in Jamacia, where he waited for a year before finding a ship to take him back to Spain. After his return he entered into a conflict with the Spanish crown when he tried to collect the portion of wealth taken from the New World that had been promised to him in 1492. The legal fight continued for fifty years after his death on May 20, 1506, but his descendants were never able to collect any of the promised riches.

needed to stall the sailor—her resources and attention were almost totally devoted to the war she was waging on the Moors. But she was interested in his offer and wanted to keep him from shopping it elsewhere. Columbus tempted the queen with promises both of riches—which she could use to fund her armies—and of new peoples who could be converted to the Christian faith.

The committee appointed to review Columbus's plea was divided in its final opinion. They were mostly theologians, not astronomers or geographers. They disagreed with Columbus's estimates of the size of the Atlantic Ocean—a vast watery expanse then called the Ocean Sea, or, more ominously, the Atlantic Abyss. Some even believed that Columbus would disappear into that abyss if he attempted to carry out his plan.

Columbus engaged the committee in fierce debates. After years of frustration trying to get funding for his voyage, he had come to believe that he had been called for a divine purpose. Isabella may have perceived this confidence as a sign that Columbus was right. She kept him on retainer, stringing him along, giving him just enough to live on for two years while the committee held more meetings.

Over the next few years, Columbus continued to appeal to Ferdinand and Isabella. He scrounged a living selling maps and taking loans from the rich friends he made in Castile. He never gave up on his quest for funds for exploration even though, in 1489, Talavera offered his opinion that it "did not conform with the dignity of such great princes to support a project resting on such weak foundations." The other committee members agreed that the proposed journey was too long and that even if Columbus could sail west to arrive in the East, they doubted he would be able to get back. Still Isabella and Ferdinand did not reject

Columbus completely. When they eventually stopped his allowance, they gave him a letter asking all Castilian innkeepers to grant him free room and board.

Late in the summer of 1491, forty-year-old Columbus again pressed his plea to the royal couple. If they would fund his trip, he insisted

This painting shows Columbus in discussion with the physicist Garcia Hernandez. The first known globe was created in 1492, the same year Columbus set forth on his trip, so, despite this picture, it is unlikely that the sailor actually ever saw a globe before his first journey.

again, he would find a western route to the Orient that would bring them all great riches and also new opportunities to spread Christianity. He presented his maps and theories to a different committee, this one made up mostly of astronomers, mariners, and pilots. Columbus, however, was less patient than he had been before. He believed deeply that he was bestowing a favor on Isabella and Ferdinand and that they should thank him, not question him. He decided to give the royal couple only a little more time. If they did not sponsor him, he would appeal to Charles VIII of France who, he said, would treat him more generously.

The timing of Columbus's latest request coincided with the Castilian capture of Granada. Anticipating the end of the expensive war, Isabella was finally willing to fund the journey Columbus so fervently hoped would lead to riches and fame. After three more months of negotiations, Columbus signed the papers. In addition to the funds he needed, Columbus insisted that he would be both viceroy and *almirante,* admiral, of all the lands he discovered. Though it was unusual to grant a common seaman such elevated status, Isabella conceded this point. She insisted, however, that Columbus could keep only one-tenth of all the wealth

This engraving by Theodore de Bry from 1594 depicts Isabella and Ferdinand bidding farewell to Columbus as he departs from the Spanish coast on August 3, 1492 on his first journey. Behind Columbus, the crew of ninety men are boarding the three ships that would take this expedition to the New World.

he found—the rest would go to the crown.

Their business settled, Isabella and Ferdinand gave Columbus a letter of safe conduct that stated he was "on some business that touches the service of God and the expansion of the Catholic Faith and our own benefit and utility." He was provided with three ships, called caravels, which would sail under the Castilian flag. The ships, the *Niña*, the *Pinta*, and the *Santa María*, carried a year's supply of food and a crew of ninety who were not afraid of sea monsters or of dropping off the edge of the earth. On August 3, 1492, the three ships set out.

The winter of 1492 and the succeeding spring were flourishing, heady times for Isabella, Ferdinand, and their subjects. Their kingdoms were at peace for the first time. Peasants freed from the burden of war plowed fields and planted crops. Blacksmiths made plows and scythes instead of swords and bullets. Millers ground wheat for civilian, not military, consumption. Shepherds grazed their sheep without fear of attack or confiscation. The Christian people of newly united Spain viewed their king and queen as gifts from God.

While Columbus was gone, Isabella and Ferdinand focused on strengthening the economy. They reformed the system of collecting taxes and other levies. They limited the export of some goods like cereal and iron in order to make them available to the citizens. They promoted shipbuilding, both because it was vital to military defense and because it was a profitable business. They licensed a guild for the production and exportation of wool, a highly valuable commodity in the newly developing textile industry. In all her actions and statements, Isabella reminded citizens of their religious duties as well as their civic responsibilities. She even attempted to reform the church by publicly attacking fraud and corruption as well as indolence and sexual promiscuity within the church hierarchy. The royal couple considered sexual sins, especially sodomy, equivalent to high treason. Isabella and Ferdinand had established a powerful, absolute monarchy. The king and queen made the final decisions in every aspect of government.

Ferdinand was especially interested in foreign affairs. Having sent Columbus off in search of new lands, the Catholic rulers turned their attention to the region around them. They wanted to advance both their government and their religion into Africa. The Canary Islands, located in the Atlantic Ocean off the northwest coast of Africa, had long been a bone of contention between Portugal and Castile. Without consulting or informing Portugal, Ferdinand and Isabella set up offices in the Canary Islands and in western Africa to collect customs duties. Despite initial resistance from the native populations, Spain soon was able to exploit the natural resources of the area.

Once firmly under Castilian control, the Canaries became a model for how Spain would conquer, explore, and exploit its colonies in North and South America. Ferdinand and Isabella implemented a system in which private individuals assumed much of the risk—and the reward—for exploration. The monarchs could not afford to empty the government's treasury on expeditions, but they could en-

Columbus was received at the Spanish court as a hero after his first voyage. Here he is depicted showing Isabella and Ferdinand his collection of Caribbean natives, tools, weapons, and exotic animals. *(National History Museum, Buenos Aires)*

courage rich citizens to fund excursions with promises to let them reap financial and political rewards, as long as Spain, and the crown, benefited. The highly organized and efficient government the king and queen had set up in Castile was copied abroad. Expansion was quick, effective, and ruthless. When questioned about these extensions of her authority, Isabella replied that she was doing God's work as well as the work of the Spanish government.

In March of 1493, less than a year after he had set out,

Columbus returned to Spain with the news that he had discovered a passageway to the Orient. He was greeted with pomp in the great hall of the old palace at Barcelona. He brought back cotton, cinnamon, some small animals much like rabbits, monkeys, and many other strange and exotic specimens. He also brought back six Native Americans, who he thought were from India, that Isabella was pleased to see baptized. His only disappointment was that he had not managed to find the gold he had hoped would be there.

It later became clear that Columbus had not, in fact, discovered a new route to the Indies but had instead stumbled upon the outlying islands of a new land mass. Though he would make three more trips across the ocean, Columbus would never find the riches and glory that had fueled his dreams.

In 1493, however, these disappointments were still in the future. Columbus still believed—and was able to convince Isabella—that his success meant God approved of the exploration: "His Divine Majesty does all good things . . . nothing can be imagined or planned without His consent. This voyage has miraculously proven this to be so." Eager to establish a Spanish colony in this new world, Isabella urged Columbus to set sail again as soon as possible to make further claims for Spain. The royal couple felt doubly blessed. With the conquest of Granada and Columbus's discoveries, Spain had vanquished the Muslims within the country and was now better able to convert the people they thought of as heathens in the Indies.

Isabella and Ferdinand moved quickly to establish their

right to the lands that Columbus discovered. When Columbus returned from his first trip, he had been forced by bad weather to land first in Portugal. Once he learned where Columbus had been, the Portuguese king, it was rumored, had immediately begun planning an expedition of his own. Isabella and Ferdinand sent an ambassador to Portugal to ask him to respect the Castilian claim to Columbus's discoveries. The Portuguese king responded by reminding them of the Treaty of Alcacovas that, when signed in 1479, stipulated that Portugal was entitled to all lands west of Africa and south of the Canary Islands.

In order to ensure their claims, Isabella and Ferdinand sent word to Pope Alexander VI of Columbus's discoveries, and pressured him to grant them sovereignty over these new territories. The pope had the authority to do so because he was the highest-ranking official in the Christian world. He was also indebted to Isabella and Ferdinand, and despite the protests from Portugal, he issued a bull confirming their right to the new land.

Not wishing to antagonize the Portuguese any further, Isabella and Ferdinand proposed dividing the globe up between them. The Casa de Tratado de Tordesillas was a treaty designed to solve the problem. Castile would be able to keep its claims to the New World, but anything below a specific latitude would belong to Portugal. Six years after the treaty was signed, a Portuguese explorer claimed what is now Brazil. Historians have debated since whether the Portuguese had already suspected it existed and managed to use the Tordesillas treaty to trick Castile.

This engraving depicts Columbus landing in the Bahamas and immediately claiming the island in the name of the king and queen of Spain.

Once the question of authority had been decided, Isabella and Ferdinand set about equipping Columbus for another voyage. This time he was to take enough people and supplies to establish a colony. Columbus gathered seventeen ships, a crew of twelve hundred, and a vast amount of supplies, including arms and tools, cheeses, rice, chickens, cattle, goats, and pigs, as well as the seeds of oranges, lemons, and melons. Once they landed, the new settlers were to set about converting whatever natives they found to Christianity. Isabella specifically instructed Columbus to "treat the said Indians very well and lovingly." He left Spain in late 1493. This second trip lasted almost three years.

Columbus encountered almost overwhelming difficulties in the New World. The humid weather wreaked havoc on his supplies, and his men were felled by mysterious and devastating illnesses. Columbus, while a visionary and a determined explorer, was a miserable administrator. The colonies he established soon degenerated into hostile relationships with the native population. Despite Isabella's explicit direction that they were to treat indigenous people with respect, Columbus and his deputies ruled harshly. In some villages, sailors took food without paying, raped the women, and enslaved or killed the men.

Columbus himself suffered from several serious illnesses, but it is unlikely he would, or could, have prevented these abuses. Most disappointing of all for the explorer was that he never found the vast quantities of gold that he had promised to Ferdinand and Isabella as recompense for their support. When he returned to Spain, it was again as a supplicant, petitioning Ferdinand and Isabella for funds for yet another journey. The money was granted, but with it came a stern warning from Isabella. She heard about sailors

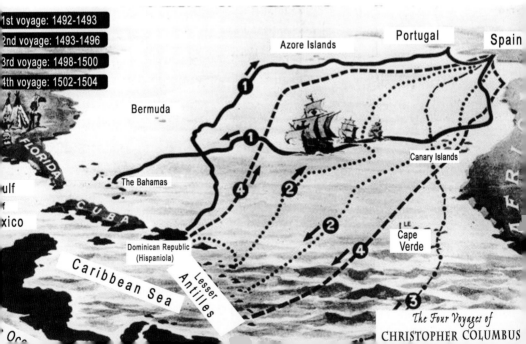

1st voyage: 1492-1493
2nd voyage: 1493-1496
3rd voyage: 1498-1500
4th voyage: 1502-1504

Azore Islands   Portugal   Spain

Bermuda

FLORIDA

Canary Islands

The Bahamas

ulf
f
xico

CUBA

Dominican Republic
(Hispaniola)

Cape
Verde

AFRICA

Caribbean Sea

Lesser Antilles

The Four Voyages of
CHRISTOPHER COLUMBUS

This engraving shows Columbus shackled in chains when he was forced to return to Spain.

taking natives as slaves, and she told Columbus that she would not abide the establishment of a slave trade. While she wanted to see the native population converted to Christianity, she would not allow it to be done by force.

Columbus set off on his third journey, from which he would return in chains after being arrested for his cruel treatment of the natives and poor administration of the colonies he had established. He was a controversial figure during his life and continues to be so today. As for the monarchs who funded his trips, though they did not see the immediate advantages of Columbus's discoveries in their lifetimes, they have always been remembered as the ones who were willing to take a risk on an unknown but determined explorer.

The next century would be an era of Spanish exploration. The country that the Catholic monarchs had united by blood and violence would, for a short while, be the most powerful in Europe as it reaped the wealth seized in newly discovered lands. For better or worse, a new era had begun, and it had been ushered in by Isabella and Ferdinand.

9

The Question of Succession

At the same time Ferdinand and Isabella were funding Columbus's expedition, they were also working to extend Spain's influence in Europe. Though the various kingdoms and provinces of the region were not yet officially united as one, they were beginning to be thought of, both at home and abroad, as Spain. Previously, when they had been merely an assortment of small kingdoms consumed with internal conflicts and problems getting along with each other, it had been impossible for any of the individual kingdoms to exert much influence in European affairs. That could change now. Ferdinand had not given up his dream of taking back control of the former Aragónese possessions, Roussillon and Cerdagne, from hated France.

For nearly twenty years, Ferdinand had been using his diplomatic power and charm to garner allies against France.

In the end, he succeeded in gaining the territory he wanted without having to go to war. In 1493, Charles VIII, the king of France, was preparing to invade Italy. Charles knew that Ferdinand would be quick to capitalize on France's distraction and would attack France from the west. He decided to cede the territory to Ferdinand rather than risk having to fight two wars.

In the middle of the treaty signing ceremony, held in Barcelona, a man darted from the crowd and thrust a dagger into the back of Ferdinand's neck. Fortunately, Ferdinand was wearing a heavy gold chain that saved his life, although the dagger left a wound four inches deep and six inches wide. When Isabella heard the news, she rushed to his side. Always practical, she also sent soldiers to protect their son Juan, in case Ferdinand should die. His prognosis did not look good.

All of Barcelona was quiet as citizens attended special masses around the clock to pray for the king. He seemed to improve for a few days but then began to run a high fever. His doctors discovered that the dagger had severed part of his shoulder bone. The court physicians had no choice but to remove the loose bone fragment—without the benefit of any anesthesia. Citizens continued to pray. Isabella bore the strain as well as could be expected. Their marriage had survived the deaths of two children and endured many long separations, but neither of them had ever had to face the possibility of losing the other. Despite the many battles Ferdinand had fought, he had always returned to her. Now, Isabella could only watch as her husband lay dying. Then, just as quickly as the assassin's knife had pierced his skin, Ferdinand began to show signs of recovery. Sooner than anyone expected, he was up and about again.

To show her gratitude to God for saving Ferdinand's life, Isabella applied new zeal to her religion. She reviewed her life, focusing on her sins, real and imagined. She berated herself for her arrogance as a child, her assumption of the throne in 1474, for sending her niece La Beltraneja to a Portuguese convent, for her exile of the Jews. She begged Talavera to keep a scrupulous record of her behavior: "It will be the greatest peace in the world for me to have it. And having it, and knowing my debts, I shall labor to pay them."

Isabella resolved once again to perfect herself, her subjects, and the church in Spain. Talavera was promoted to archbishop and Isabella chose as her new confessor Francisco de Cisneros. Cisneros was an extreme Franciscan who flagellated himself daily, wore a hair shirt next to his skin, and slept on the ground with a piece of wood for his pillow. Besides his responsibilities as confessor to Isabella, he was appointed by the pope to see that life in Spanish monasteries returned to the discipline of medieval monastic life. He demanded that monks rid themselves of all worldly possessions, forbade the serving of rich foods, and prohibited them from wearing costly clothes. Any monk who would not obey these new rules was ordered to leave.

Isabella shared in the goal of disciplining the religious community by focusing on the convents. But she took a different tack than Cisneros did with the monasteries. She resolved to change behavior by setting an example. In her visits, she dressed modestly, prayed and ate with the nuns, and spoke earnestly to them about the value of deep religious commitment.

Francisco de Cisneros.

Ferdinand and Isabella had acquiesced to the French invasion of Italy in order to win back Roussillon and Cerdagne. But when the French king Charles VIII crowned himself emperor of Naples, the Castilian monarchs could no longer turn a blind eye. Their loyalty to the pope demanded that they attempt to rescue Italy from French domination. Isabella and Ferdinand sent forces to Italy to fight against the French. The war lasted seven months. Eventually, Spanish forces gained the upper hand and the French retreated for home. Ferdinand's military prowess was confirmed, and he was able to claim Naples and Sicily for Spain. Spain was becoming an important international power.

As was the custom of the times, Ferdinand and Isabella used their children to create and maintain alliances with other countries. Isabella's first daughter, Isabel, had been married to Prince Afonso, the heir to the Portuguese throne.

This marriage was arranged in 1490, eleven years after the war of succession fought between Afonso's grandfather and Ferdinand and Isabella.

The marriage was designed to unite Portugal, Aragón, and Castile. Although the Holy War had been an enormous drain on the treasury, Isabella spared no expense for her eldest and favorite daughter's wedding. All of Seville was decorated with flowers and silk banners. For fifteen days and nights public festivals, banquets, and parades continued from early morning through the night. After the official betrothal ceremony, Isabella began wedding preparations in earnest. Hundreds of dresses and headdresses had to be ordered, and a magnificent trousseau was assembled for the bride. The dowry included a huge collection of jewels and precious stones as well as money.

After the betrothal ceremony, Isabel became the princess of Portugal. Twenty-one years earlier, the wedding of Isabella and Ferdinand had sealed a political alliance. Now Isabel and Afonso would do the same. The wedding, as was customary, would take place in Portugal. Isabella and Ferdinand were not expected to attend. Isabel's departure was sad—mother and daughter had been very close, and Isabella had relied on her daughter for support and comfort at the endless rounds of official events. Now Princess Juana became her mother's most frequent companion. Juana and Isabella were not as close—the young princess was moody and quick to show a temper.

Not long after the wedding, tragic news arrived from the Portuguese court. Princess Isabel's husband had died after being thrown from a horse. Dressed in sackcloth and with her blond hair newly shorn, the grieving young widow traveled to Andalusia to mourn in privacy. She swore that she would never marry again. Her only desire in life was to become a nun.

The question of inheritance of the twin thrones of Castile and Aragón was always on Isabella's mind. She had arranged for the engagement of her son Prince Juan to Navarre's child-queen Catalina as a way to add Navarre to the throne of Castile and Aragón. But Juan was not a healthy child, and Isabella worried that he would not live long enough to inherit the throne. Because Aragón still followed Salic Law, only a male heir would be able to claim the crown when Ferdinand died. Juan was extremely important to the future of the kingdom.

Isabella took care to educate all of her children. Juan, as the only boy, also learned to ride, hunt, play chess and cards, sing, and recite po-

After the death of her husband Afonso, Princess Isabel was so wracked with grief that she entered a convent.

etry. Because he was waited on hand and foot, Isabella worried that he was growing up selfish. She often tested his generosity by ordering him to give some of his luxurious possessions to his servants. She displayed the same aversion to luxury in her orders to court nobles and *grandees,* whom she scolded for their lavish displays of wealth. She told them, as she had told Juan, that ostentation was "without purpose . . . especially in time of war for the [poor] example it set" for the less wealthy and for its distraction from their holy mission. Isabella worked to install this same honor, strict behavior, and religious purpose in her armies. Still, always conscious of the importance of appearances, she wore her grandest gowns and jewelry at public events.

Praying for the best, Isabella brought Juan up to become a king in service to Spain and to the church. She scheduled his daily routines to include attending mass and reciting prayers before his lessons. From age ten, Juan sat in on judicial proceedings at court. In 1490, twelve-year-old Prince Juan knelt before his father, swore allegiance to God and to the king of Castile and Aragón, and became a knight. Now he was considered old enough to fight in war. Isabella hung a sword over his bed, as a constant reminder that his goal was to fight for God and his country.

Ferdinand and Isabella looked forward to Spain becoming the most powerful country in Europe. The marriages of their children seemed to foreordain this. Prince Juan would inherit a united Spain and an empire that extended overseas. Marriages of the princesses into the English ruling family and the Hapsburgs, who controlled the huge Holy Roman

Empire in Central Europe, would strengthen their connections to other power centers.

Princess Catalina, born in 1485, was the youngest of Ferdinand and Isabella's children. Soon after her birth, King Henry VII of England, the first Tudor king, proposed a pact under which England and Castile would pledge to defend each other against France if necessary. To seal the agreement, Princess Catalina would marry Henry's then-infant son Prince Arthur when they came of age. The signing ceremony was a glorious affair. Kings, queens, and infants wore the most gorgeous clothes they had with lots of sable, huge diamonds and rubies, ermine, satin, and velvet. There was little omen of the arduous future Catalina faced in England.

Having cemented an alliance with England, Isabella and Ferdinand entertained other offers of marriage for their remaining children. After Ferdinand sent troops to Italy to oust Charles VIII, he wanted to ensure the continued cooperation of Maximilian I, the Holy Roman Emperor, who was engaged in an ongoing conflict with France. Maximilian happened to have an eligible son, the Archduke Philip, and, as Isabella astutely observed, "there is not at present a King in the world who has a daughter to whom he can marry his son except ours." Princess Juana was duly betrothed. Maximilian also had a daughter, Princess Margaret, who was promised to Prince Juan.

In August, Princess Juana sailed to Flanders, a region between France and Belgium, to marry Archduke Philip. Isabella had supervised the travel preparations, including review of the 130-boat fleet that would carry the trunkloads of dresses, shoes, furniture, and jewels. They also took two hundred cattle, two thousand eggs, chickens, and casks of wine. After the send-off, there was no news from Juana for some time.

Isabella was anxious about her daughter. The young woman was temperamental and high strung. There had long been rumors about her unusual behavior. She was often compared to Isabella's own mother, who had gone mad. Three months passed before Isabella received an answer to her many letters and messages to Juana and others at the Flemish court. The answer was the simple statement that the Spanish fleet had arrived in Flanders. Later that winter, she received another short note saying that Juana was married.

A few months later, Isabella and Ferdinand greeted Princess Margaret of Flanders, who was to marry Prince Juan. The seventeen-year-old princess was charming and beautiful. Isabella graced her with lavish gifts of diamonds and emeralds and other jewels as well as elaborate furnishings of tapestries, serving dishes, and gold-covered quilts. The palace celebrated the wedding with great pomp and extravagance.

Soon after Juan's marriage, her parents convinced Princess Isabel that it was her familial and religious duty to leave the convent and marry again. She finally agreed to marry King Manuel of Portugal. He had fallen in love with her when she married Afonso, his nephew, and once he was crowned he asked for her hand. Though Isabel still grieved over the death of her first husband, the wedding that took place in 1497 dangled the tantalizing prospect that between Juan, who would rule Castile and Aragón, and Isabel's descendants, who would rule Portugal, the entire Iberian Peninsula would finally be united.

Then, just six months after his wedding, nineteen-year-old Prince Juan caught a fever and died.

Prince Juan's death came as a horrible

Prince Juan in his tomb.

blow to Isabella. She prayed and tried to stave off what she knew was the sin of despair, but she never recovered from her grief. All of Spain mourned with her. Throughout the court, men and women dressed in black sackcloth. All offices in Castile and Aragón were closed for forty days. Cities draped their buildings with black banners. Any hope of keeping Castile and Aragón united died when the widowed Princess Margaret delivered a stillborn girl a few months later.

Isabella and Ferdinand tried to proceed with the affairs of state, but their grief overwhelmed them. Isabella commissioned a great Gothic church in Toledo with beautiful stained glass windows and magnificent statues to commemorate her son. She turned to her confessor, Cisneros, to help her deal with her loss. He suggested initiating a program of clerical reform, and she agreed without hesitation. Isabella's faith allowed her to believe she could make some good from her son's death by atoning for her own sins.

Juan's death, and the subsequent death of his child, brought the question of inheritance to the fore. Archduke Philip took advantage of the confusion to declare that he and Juana were now the heirs to Castile. Isabella sent him a message rebuking him for such arrogance. She summoned her daughter, Queen Isabel, and her husband King Manuel, from Portugal. Isabel had been declared the heir to Castile before her brother Juan was born. Now, after his death, the title reverted to her, as their oldest child.

Isabel, in turn, informed her parents that she was pregnant. Isabella was delighted—she and Manuel could claim the twin thrones of Castile and Aragón for their unborn child and the possibility of a united peninsula would still exist. But tragedy intervened, again. Isabel delivered a baby boy, but both mother and child died in childbirth.

This loss was almost more than Isabella and Ferdinand could stand. They isolated themselves and mourned the death of another child. There was no news from Juana, not even when others reported first that she was pregnant and, later, that she had delivered a baby girl.

Isabella would later discover that she had made a bad match for Juana. Philip was a rake—a drunkard and a libertine. Despite his cold abusivenes, Juana had fallen completely in love with her husband. She was fiercely jealous of his lovers, and her actions became increasingly

Princess Juana's husband, Philip the Handsome. *(Courtesy of Art Resource.)*

incoherent as his cruelty threatened her sanity.

Isabella might have seen these problems as a punishment from God for her sins. Was it because she had failed to completely rid the country of non-Catholics? She directed

Cisneros and Talavera to speed the process of conversions in Spain, ignoring protests from the pope that the Spanish Inquisition was out of control. Cisneros broke the terms of the 1492 treaty under which he had pledged that Granada would be safe from the Inquisition for forty years. His agents began to question, persecute, and kill Moors.

They removed thousands of beautifully embossed Arabic manuscripts from mosques and libraries in Granada, destroying eight centuries of Moorish culture in the process. Cisneros ordered the burning of hand-copied manuscripts of the Koran and other religious texts. The Moors retaliated by killing two of Cisneros's men and storming his palace. The hard-won stability in Granada was on the verge of turning into rebellion. When Ferdinand heard about the situation, he was angry, saying "We are like to pay dear for our Archbishop [Cisneros], whose rashness has lost us in a few hours what we have been years in acquiring."

By December 1499, priests were gathering large crowds in public squares and ordering them to lie prostrate on the ground. They would then sprinkle holy water from balconies, baptizing thousands at a time. Inevitably, some citizens revolted against these forced conversions—even though many Muslims appeared to be sincere in their desire to join the Catholic faith. Ferdinand and Isabella retaliated by pressing the issue further. They announced that, because the Muslim revolts violated the treaty of 1492, all remaining Muslim residents of Granada would either convert or be exiled. Their ploy worked. Thousands of Muslims professed to convert, and peace was soon restored to the newly

Christian kingdom. Given what happened when the Spanish rulers had forcibly converted the Jewish population, it should come as no surprise that a hundred years later the Muslims were eventually expelled from the kingdom. Like the *conversos*, they were first persecuted for attempting to maintain their own faith, then persecuted again after abandoning it. And like the *conversos,* many were killed before the population as a whole was expelled.

Isabella and Ferdinand made one last attempt to unite the Iberian Peninsula. They married their last daughter, Maria, to the Portuguese King Manuel, Princess Isabel's widower, in 1500. But Maria, as well, would die young, at the age of thirty-five.

Princess Catalina, better known as Catherine of Aragón. *(Kunsthistorisches Museum, Vienna.)*

In the spring of 1501, fifteen-year-old Catalina and fourteen-year-old Prince Arthur of England were finally old enough to fulfill the marriage pact arranged for them so many years before. Catalina's departure was particularly sad for Isabella who was

Catalina's second husband, the infamous King Henry VIII of England.

close to this daughter. She had already experienced so much grief from the marriages of Isabel, Juan, and Juana. Isabella advised King Henry VII: "We, therefore beg the King, our brother, to moderate the expenses. Rejoicings may be held, but we ardently implore him that the substantial part of the festival should be his love." Pretty and personable Catalina married Prince Arthur in November of 1501. Known to history as Catherine of Aragón, she would, upon the death of Arthur, marry his younger brother, the future King Henry VIII. She would bear and lose six children, each before their second birthdays. Eventually her husband would divorce her, an act that led to a schism with the Catholic Church and the creation of the Church of England.

Soon after Catherine left Spain, Juana and Philip arrived in Castile, in January of 1501. They came to cement their claim to the thrones of Castile and Aragón. Isabella and Ferdinand welcomed them uncertainly. They had heard the rumors about Philip's abuse of Juana, and they were not happy to think he would one day rule their kingdom.

Philip and Juana had not been in Castile long before news arrived that Prince Arthur had died. Sixteen-year-old Catherine was a widow. The gay festivities planned for Philip and Juana were subdued. Isabella's health was troubling her. She was now over fifty and suffered from painful swelling in her legs.

Ferdinand and Isabella decided they had to address the question of succession. Ferdinand presided at a meeting of the *cortes* to make sure that Juana was recognized as the heir to both Castile and Aragón. He added the stipulation that if Isabella died and Ferdinand remarried, any male child he had would take precedence over Juana. The problem, as always, was that Castile did not follow Salic Law while Aragón did.

Philip was not happy about this arrangement. To show his disdain, and to escape what he thought was a boring and overly religious court, he announced that he had to return to Flanders on important business. Juana, who was seven months pregnant, could not travel with him. His leaving tortured her; she was convinced he was fleeing to the arms of a mistress. Though they were happy to see him go, both Ferdinand and Isabella tried to convince him to stay for their daughter's sake. Philip could not be swayed and Juana was alone save for her mother when she gave birth to a boy she called Charles. It was also becoming apparent that Juana suffered from something more severe than what we today call postpartum depression. She tried several times to escape the castle, leaving her newborn behind, in order to reach her husband.

Isabella dealt with her daughter as best she could, but she collapsed under the stress and exhaustion. She ran a high fever and suffered severe pains in her side. Her doctors suggested that Juana was the cause of Isabella's illness. "We believe that the Queen's life is endangered by her contact with Madame Princess who staged scenes every day," they reported. Isabella spent the summer in and out of her sickbed. When she was able, she took care of her duties and tried to cope with Juana. Philip ignored repeated letters and messages to come to visit his wife and son.

Juana told her parents she could no longer stand to live

Princess Juana became known as Juana La Loca, or "Juana the Mad."

under their roof. Against their wishes, she moved out. As soon as she was away from her parents' control she made plans to return to Philip. Though Isabella and Ferdinand posted guards, she tried to bolt from the castle one night, barefoot and half-dressed. The guards caught her trying to open a heavy iron gate. They tried to subdue her but she fought them. Surrounded by the guards, the half-naked princess paced back and forth behind the gate as dumbfounded citizens gathered to stare. The story quickly spread, and the people began to call her *Juana La Loca,* or Juana the Mad.

Isabella and Ferdinand were devastated by their daughter's loss of sanity. They knew that she would eventually sneak back to Philip. The thrones of Castile and Aragón would one day be under the control of their despised son-in-law. The only thing Isabella could do was to write to Philip begging him to be kind to Juana and to ask Juana's attendants to keep her from hurting herself or others.

It weighed heavily on Isabella and Ferdinand that the kingdom they had worked so hard to create would be lost when they died. It was increasingly obvious that Philip would one day take the throne. They knew he had no interest in maintaining the glory of Spain.

As if her body was reflecting the despair she felt in her mind, Isabella developed a thirst that could not be quenched and ran a fever the doctors could not break. Her body swelled with retained water. By September 1504, her health was so precarious her court wondered openly who would be her successor. Under the terms of their marriage contract,

Ferdinand could not rule Castile after Isabella's death. The throne would go to Juana the Mad.

Isabella knew that she was dying and worked with all her remaining strength to prepare her soul. She called on God and the Virgin Mary as well as her favorite saints to accept her. She affirmed her belief that God had singled her out for special suffering to test her. She hoped she had passed the tests. She worried about her judgment by Jesus: "And if none can justify themselves before Him, how much less can we of great kingdoms and estates who have to give account?" She asked that her body be interred, wearing a nun's habit, in a simple tomb in the Franciscan monastery in Granada. She requested that her funeral be simple and that the money customarily spent on funeral wakes and masses be given to the poor. With no other options, she designated Juana as her heir, "conforming with what I ought to do and am obliged by law."

On October 12, bedridden Queen Isabella signed her will. She left pensions to faithful servants, donations to the poor and widows and orphans, and willed household goods to convents and hospitals. She made provisions for Ferdinand to receive income from Castile. She also left him her jewels with a note that confirmed she was "waiting for him in a better world." She asked that Ferdinand be buried next to her and added a last desperate clause to her will. The provision stated that if Juana was unwilling or unable to take over the throne, Ferdinand would be named regent until their grandson Charles turned twenty and could take over. The clause was designed to keep Castile from Philip, and to give

In this nineteenth-century painting by Eduardo Rosales, Queen Isabella is depicted on her deathbed, signing her will. Hunched in a chair beside her is Ferdinand, with Princess Juana standing behind him. In the group on the right is the covered figure of Cardinal Cisneros. *(The Prado Museum, Madrid.)*

Ferdinand the chance to keep the peninsula whole.

As she withered away, she told faithful friends and aides, "Do not weep for me, nor waste your time in fruitless recovery. But pray for my soul." On November 26, 1504, fifty-three-year-old Isabella received all the sacraments, made the sign of the cross, and died. It fell to her loyal husband to inform their subjects that her reign was over. "We may believe that Our Lord has received her into His glory, that is a greater and more lasting kingdom than any here on earth," he wrote.

When Philip learned of Isabella's death he tried to contest the provision in her will ceding power to Ferdinand until

QUEEN ISABELLA'S DEATHBED INSTRUCTIONS TO THE GOVERNMENT REGARDING THE TREATMENT OF INDIANS

November 26, 1504

Whereas, when the islands and mainland of the Ocean Sea were conceded to us by the Holy Apostolic See, our principal intention . . . was to procure, induce, bring, and convert their peoples to our Holy Catholic Faith and to send to the said islands and maintain bishops, religious, clerics and other learned and God fearing persons, to instruct the inhabitants and dwellers therein in the Catholic Faith, and to instruct them in, and to bestow upon them, good customs, exercising all proper diligence in this therefore, I beg the King my Lord very affectionately, and I charge and command my said daughter (Juana) and the said prince her husband (Philip I) to carry this out, and that it be their principal purpose, and that they put into it much diligence: and they are not to consent, or give permission, that the Indian inhabitants and dwellers in the said islands and mainland . . . receive any damage in their persons or goods, but are to order that they be well and justly treated, and if they have received any damage it is to be remedied: and it is to be provided that everything enjoined and commanded us in the said concession be strictly observed.

Isabella's wishes would not be respected. This painting shows the Spanish explorer Hernán Cortés engaged in warfare against the Aztecs in the mid-1500s.

Charles came of age. The two men battled for supremacy until Philip died two years later. Ferdinand continued the work he and Isabella had done, making Spain a dominant power in Europe.

After Ferdinand died in 1516, Juana and Philip's son Charles V (known as Carlos I in Spain) locked his mother in a cell and forced her to sign papers of abdication. Charles had inherited Spain and its colonies, the Netherlands, Austria, half of Italy, and some German principalities. He soon was elected to the office of Holy Roman Emperor, which made him the most powerful ruler in Europe. No other ruler, including Napoleon and Hitler, has ever controlled a larger area in Europe. Charles's reign saw a tremendous increase in the power of the Spanish empire, though it also endured many expensive and bloody wars. The dismantling of his holdings was begun when Charles parceled off lands to his children as they married.

The Iberian Peninsula was briefly united, as Ferdinand and Isabella had dreamed, from 1580-1640. Charles V gave the kingdom of Spain to his son, Philip II. Philip used superior force to overcome the tenuousness of his claim to the throne of Portugal, and for sixty years the two countries were governed as one. By the time the Portuguese mounted a successful revolt and regained their independence, much of the enormous territory they had won had been lost. Portugal would keep its sovereignty, but never again wield tremendous power on a global scale.

The Catholic monarchs left a powerful legacy, shaping the future of Spain for many years. Catholicism was the

official state religion until 1978, and the country has a monarchy to this day—albeit one guided primarily by a constitution. The Spanish Inquisition continued long after Ferdinand and Isabella were dead, reaching the zenith of its power and influence in the sixteenth century under Philip II. A series of draining wars and political instability weakened the country over the next three hundred years, and internal dissension led to a monumental civil war in 1936. Spain became a dictatorship under General Francisco Franco, a condition that was maintained until the late 1970s. Even now, separatist movements continue to threaten the stability of the state. The unification Ferdinand and Isabella worked so hard to achieve is still, it seems, not complete.

Opposite: A portrait of Charles V on horseback by the Italian painter Titian. *(The Prado Museum, Madrid)*

Timeline

1451	Isabella is born in Castile.
1468	Rejects throne.
1469	Marries Ferdinand.
1470	Gives birth to Isabel.
1474	Accepts throne after Enrique's death.
1476	Imposes stability and reform in Castile.
late 1470s	Strips *grandees* of much of their power.
1478	Gives birth to Juan.
1479	Gives birth to Juana.
1480s	Carries out Inquisition.
1481	Declares war on Granada.
1482	Quarrels with pope about Spanish Inquisition; gives birth to Maria.
1485	Gives birth to Catalina.
1491	Accepts surrender of Granada.
1492	Sends Columbus on his explorations; signs Edict of Expulsion against Jews.
1493	Nurses Ferdinand after assassination attempt.
1504	Dies on November 26.

TIMELINE FOR SPAIN

1000 B.C.E.	Phoenicians colonize Spain.
400 B.C.E.	Carthaginians conquer much of Spain.
200 B.C.E.	Romans take Spain from Carthaginians.
C.E. 400	Visigoths take Spain from Romans.
711	Moors conquer almost all of Spain.
1000s	Christians begin to drive Moors from Spain.
1479	Aragón and Castile united.
1492	Spanish forces conquer Granada.
1512	King Ferdinand V seizes Navarre which completes unification of present-day Spain.
1588	English navy defeats the Spanish armada.
1808	Napoleon seizes Madrid.
1808-14	French are driven from Spain.
1800s	Spain loses all of its American colonies.
1931	Spain becomes a democratic republic.
1936-39	Spanish Civil war; dictator General Francisco Franco comes to power.
1975	Spaniards set up new democratic government when Franco dies.
1982	Spain joins North Atlantic Treaty Organization.
1986	Spain becomes part of the European Community.
1992	Spain celebrates the 500th anniversary of unification; Olympic Games held in Barcelona.

Glossary

almirante Admiral.

anti-Semitism Hostility/prejudice toward Jews.

auto-da-fe "Act of faith," a term for the trial of accused heretics.

caravel Small, light sailing ship.

confessor Priest who hears confession and gives absolution.

converso A person of another faith who has converted to Christianity.

cortes Legislative body.

dispensation Exemption from church law.

grandee Wealthy noble.

heresy Dissension from traditional Christian beliefs.

hermandad Police force.

Iberian Peninsula Region of southwestern Europe.

Inquisition Investigation, trial, and punishment of non-Christians conducted by the Catholic Church.

Moor A Muslim of Arabian or African descent.

papal bull Official document issued by the Pope.

pogrom An organized, often officially encouraged massacre or persecution of a minority group, especially one conducted against Jews.

quemadero A field in which heretics were burned.

reconquista The reconquest of Spain from Moors.

Renaissance Fourteenth- and fifteenth-century cultural movement focused on learning and the arts.

siege Blockading of a town to keep it from getting supplies.

Tanto monta, monta tanto "One is equal to the other."

Sources

CHAPTER ONE: A Weak King

p. 17, "dear and much loved sister" Nancy Rubin, *Isabella of Castile: The First Renaissance Queen* (New York: St. Martin's Press, 1991), 48.

CHAPTER TWO: Lies and Betrayals

p. 24, "From the hand which . . ." Rubin, *Isabella of Castile,* 69.

p. 29, "God will make you. . . ." Ibid., 98.

CHAPTER THREE: Crowning a Queen

p. 40, "We are going to avenge . . ." Rubin, *Isabella of Castile,* 112.

p. 40, "Death to the *conversos!*" Peggy Liss, *Isabel the Queen* (New York: Oxford University Press, 1992),164.

p. 46, "Castile, Castile, for the Queen . . ." Rubin, *Isabella of Castile,* 5.

p. 47, "obey and receive His Highness . . ." Liss, *Isabel the Queen,* 104.

p. 49, "this subject [succession], Lord . . ." William Thomas Walsh, *Isabella of Spain: The Last Crusader* (New York: Robert M. McBride & Company, 1930), 97.

CHAPTER FOUR: Uniting Spain

p. 51, "My Lord Jesus Christ . . ." Rubin, *Isabella of Castile*, 136.

p. 52, "I will enter my city . . ." Walsh, *Isabella of Spain*, 136.

p. 56, "The reason why you do . . ." Rubin, *Isabella of Castile*, 138.

p. 56, "If you say to me that women . . ." Liss, *Isabel the Queen*, 117.

p. 57, "If you had forced the forts open . . ." Rubin, *Isabella of Castile*, 140.

p. 57, "I thought that coming back . . ." Ibid., 141.

p. 58, "I am queen of Castile . . ." Irene Plunket, *Isabel of Castile and the Making of the Spanish Nation* (New York: G.P. Putnam's Sons, 1915), 113.

p. 60, "with the help of our Lord" Rubin, *Isabella of Castile*, 151.

p. 61, "May you give me intelligence and strength . . ." Liss, *Isabel the Queen*, 123.

p. 62, "Renew through God . . ." Ibid., 126.

CHAPTER FIVE: The Spanish Inquisition

p. 76, "to the extirpation of heresy . . ." Rubin, *Isabella of Castile,* 188.

CHAPTER SIX: War against the Moors

p. 84, "the first place . . . by all means." Walsh, *Isabella of Spain*, 239.

p. 94, "God knows our cause . . ." Rubin, *Isabella of Castile*, 243.

p. 94, "Hunger alone will . . ." Ibid., 282.

p. 96, "We assure you that this city . . ." Liss, *Isabel the Queen*, 237.

CHAPTER SEVEN: The Expulsion of the Jews
p. 98, "What is done for fear . . ." Rubin, *Isabella of Castile,* 338.

p. 101, "The Inquisition has for . . ." Ibid., 201.

p. 101, "Take care . . . [to] entrust . . ." Rubin, *Isabella of Castile,* 201.

p. 103, "to much abuse and mistreatment . . ." Ibid., 280.

p. 104, "Please, O King . . ." Ibid., 299.

p. 105, "a house [given] . . ." Plunket, *Isabel of Castile,* 268.

p. 105, "by the roads and fields . . ." Rubin, *Isabella of Castile,* 302.

CHAPTER EIGHT: Columbus
p. 108, "Our Lord revealed to me . . ." Rubin, *Isabella of Castile,* 237.

p. 112, "did not conform . . ." Ibid., 274.

p. 115, "on some business that . . ." Liss, *Isabel the Queen,* 290.

p. 118, "His Divine Majesty . . ." Rubin, *Isabella of Castile,* 330.

p. 120, "treat the said Indians . . ." Ibid., 332.

CHAPTER NINE: The Question of Succession
p. 126, "It will be the greatest peace ..." Rubin, *Isabella of Castile,* 310.

p. 130, "without purpose . . . especially . . ." Ibid., 222.

p. 131, "there is not at present . . ." Ibid., 349.

p. 136, "We are like to pay dear . . ." Ibid., 373.

p. 138, "We, therefore beg the King . . ." Ibid., 390.

p. 140, "We believe that the . . ." Ibid., 402.

p. 142, "And if none can justify . . ." Liss, *Isabel the Queen,* 345.

p. 142, "conforming with what . . ." Ibid., 347.

p. 142, "waiting for him in a . . ." Plunket, *Isabel of Castile,* 383.

p. 143, "Do not weep for me . . ." Rubin, *Isabella of Castile,* 415.

p. 143, "We may believe . . ." Plunket, *Isabel of Castile,* 385.

Bibliography

Elliott, J.H. *Imperial Spain 1469-1716.* New York: St. Martin's Press, 1964.

Liss, Peggy. *Isabel the Queen.* New York: Oxford University Press, 1992.

Lofts, Norah. *Crown of Aloes.* New York: Doubleday & Co., 1974.

Mariejol, Jean H. *The Spain of Ferdinand and Isabella.* Trans. Benjamin Keen. New Jersey: Rutgers University Press, 1961.

McKendrick, Melveena. *The Horizon Concise History of Spain.* New York: American Heritage Publishing Co., Inc., 1972.

Plaidy, Jean. *Castile for Isabella.* London: Robert Hale, 1960.

Plunket, Irene L. *Isabel of Castile and the Making of the Spanish Nation.* New York: G.P. Putnam's Sons, 1915.

Rubin, Nancy. *Isabella of Castile: The First Renaissance Queen.* New York: St. Martin's Press, 1991.

Smith, Rhea March. *Spain: A Modern History.* Ann Arbor: The University of Michigan Press, 1965.

Walsh, William Thomas. *Isabella of Spain: The Last Crusader.* New York: Robert M. McBride & Company, 1930.

Web sites

http://womenshistory.about.com/cs/medrenqueens/p/
p_isabella_i.htm
About.com offers a profile of the queen along with links to
other resources and pictures.

http://www.d.umn.edu/~aroos/isabellapage.html
A lengthy biography, offering insight into Isabella's reign
and some illustrations.

http://www.kings.edu/womens_history/isabel.html
A brief biography and annotated bibliography from King's
College.

http://www.clevelandart.org/exhibcef/consexhib/html/
hours.html
Beautiful illustrations from and information about Queen
Isabella's famous prayer book, the Book of Hours.

http://www.usmint.gov/kids/
index.cfm?fileContents=coinNews/cotm/1999/10.cfm
A fun story about Queen Isabella's importance to American
coins.

$\mathcal{I}ndex$